A Sequential
Program for
Adults

Book Three

Program Authors

Linda Ward Beech • **James W. Beers**
Jo Ann Dauzat • **Sam V. Dauzat** • **Tara McCarthy**

Program Consultants

David C. Bub
Albany-Schoharie-Schenectady B.O.C.E.S.
Albany, New York

Christina H. Miller
Shoals Area Adult Education Program
Muscle Shoals, Alabama

Dannette S. Queen
Office of Adult and Continuing Education
New York, New York

John Ritter
Oregon Women's Correctional Center
Salem, Oregon

Lydia Smith
Adult Literacy Instructors' Training Institute
Los Angeles, California

Betty L. Walker
Richard J. Daley College
Chicago, Illinois

STECK-VAUGHN
C O M P A N Y
A Subsidiary of National Education Corporation

Acknowledgments

● ● ● ● ●

Staff Credits:

Executive Editor:	Ellen Lehrburger
Senior Supervising Editor:	Carolyn Hall
Project Editor:	Margie Weaver
Design Manager:	Donna Brawley
Electronic Production:	Kristian Polo, Shelly Knapp
Cover Design:	Pamela Heaney
Photo Editor:	Margie Foster

Photography Credits:

Mike Flahive

Kurt Johnson

James Minor

David Omer

Rick Patrick

Joel Schwartz

Rick Williams

Cover Photography:

© Comstock

Illustration Credits:

Alan Klemp, Cath Polito

ISBN: 0-8114-9220-6

Contents

Scope and Sequence

Book Title	Sight Words/Vocabulary	Phonics/Word Study
Introductory Book	• Visual discrimination of letters/words • Recognition of letters of the alphabet • Sight words in context • Question words (*who, what, when, where, why*) • 157 words total	• Initial and final consonants • Short vowels and CVC word pattern • Long vowels and CVC + *e* word pattern
Book One	• Introduces 107 sight words, function words, and number words • Reviews 143 words from the *Introductory Book*	• Letter-sound associations reviewed for 　Consonants 　Short vowels and CVC word pattern 　Long vowels and CVC + *e* word pattern
Book Two	• Sight word pages introduce 63 new words • Review word pages reinforce 143 words from the *Introductory Book* and 107 words from *Book 1*	• Short vowels taught and reviewed through these word families: 　Short *a* in *-at, -an, -ad, -and* 　Short *e* in *-end, -ent, -et, -ed* 　Short *o* in *-op, -ot* 　Short *i* in *-in, -it* 　Short *u* in *-ut, -un* • Initial consonants reviewed and recycled
Book Three	• Sight word pages introduce 63 new words • Review word pages reinforce 84 sight words from *Books 1–2*	• Long vowels taught and reviewed through these word families: 　Long *a* in *-ake, -ay* 　Long *i* in *-ine, -ight* 　Long *o* in *-ope, -old* 　Long *e* in *-eed, -eat* 　Long *u* in *-une, -ute* • Short vowels reviewed through these word families: *-ag, -ell, -ip, -ig, -ug* • Initial consonant blends introduced in context: *st, sh, wh, pr, dr, str, th, cl, tr*

# of Program Strands

Language/Writing	Comprehension/Life Skills
• Writing letters of the alphabet • Writing words and sentences • Language experience stories • Journal writing	• Finding the main idea • Recalling facts and details
• Antonyms • Adding -s to form plurals • Adding -s, -ed, and -ing endings to verbs • Writing sentences • Language experience stories • Journal writing	• Predicting • Summarizing • Recalling facts and details • Finding the main idea
• Forming plurals with -s • Adding -s, -ed, and -ing to verbs • Forming contractions • Capitalizing sentences and proper names • Adding 's to form singular possessive of nouns • Doubling the final consonant to add -ed and -ing to verbs • Writing sentences • Journal writing	• **Comprehension skills:** predicting, summarizing, recalling facts and details, finding the main idea, inferring, sequencing events, drawing conclusions, determining cause and effect • **Life skills:** managing money, moving to find work, maintaining health, using leisure time, job safety, understanding self and others, selecting a satisfying job
• Compound words • Irregular plurals • Adding -er to nouns • End punctuation of sentences • Irregular verbs • Dropping final e to add -ed and -ing to verbs • Using quotation marks in dialog • Writing sentences • Journal writing	• **Comprehension skills:** predicting, summarizing, recalling facts and details, finding the main idea, inferring, sequencing events, drawing conclusions, determining cause and effect • **Life skills:** finding ways to increase income, rearing children, promoting health care, handling social relationships, learning about training programs, coping with job dissatisfaction, working together for change

Scope and Sequence

Book Title	Sight Words/Vocabulary	Phonics/Word Study

Book Four	• Sight word pages introduce 84 new words
	• Review word pages reinforce 84 sight words from *Books 2–3*
	• Life Skill pages introduce 28 new words
		• Consonant blends taught:
		  r blends: *br, cr, dr, fr, gr, pr, str, tr*
		  s blends: *sc, sk, sm, sn, sp, st, str, sw*
		  l blends: *bl, cl, fl, gl, pl, sl*
		• Consonant digraphs taught: *ch, sh, shr, th, wh*
		• Silent letters taught: *wr, kn, gu, gh*
		• Long vowels *i* and *e* spelled *-y* taught
		• Long and short vowels reviewed through these word families: *-ay, -ack, -ank, -ate, -ean, -ear, -eep, -eet, -ight, -in, -ine, -ink, -ing, -ock, -ub, -y*
		• Syllables defined
		• Vowel sound as schwa introduced

Book Five	• Sight word pages introduce 84 new words • Review word pages reinforce 84 sight words from *Books 3–4* • Life Skill pages introduce 30 new words	• Vowel digraphs taught through these word families: *-age, -aid, -ain, -ame, -ape, -ay, -ie, -ice, -ight, -ind, -ive, -ook, -ool, -oon, -ue, -ew, -all, -aw* • Diphthongs taught through these word families: *-oil, -oy, -own, -ound, -oup, -ow* • R-controlled vowels taught through these word families: *-ark, -art, -irl, -ork, -orn, and -urse* • Consonant blends and digraphs reviewed and recycled • Syllables and schwa reviewed

Book Six	• Definition pages introduce 70 new words
	• Vocabulary pages cover the following skills:
	  Multiple meanings Suffixes
	  Word stress Prefixes
	  Antonyms Analogies
	  Dictionary entries
	• Vocabulary, word study, and life skills pages introduce new words in context
		• Dividing words into syllables using VCV, VCCV, and consonant + *le* word patterns
		• Dictionary entries
		• Dictionary pronunciations
		• Dictionary accent marks

# of Program Strands

Language/Writing	Comprehension	Life Skills
• Irregular verbs • Prefixes *re-* and *un-* • Plurals with *-ies* • Suffixes *-ly, -ful, -ness, -y* • Abbreviations and titles • Days of the week and months of the year • Journal writing	• Predicting • Summarizing • Cause and effect • Inference • Stated and implied main idea • Sequence • Context • Drawing conclusions	• Writing a letter • Reading coupons • Reading a report card • Reading a prescription • Reading park rules • Coping with shyness • Reading a schedule
• Word building skills reviewed: forming plurals; adding *-s, -ed,* and *-ing*; adding prefixes and suffixes • Adding *-er* and *-est* to adjectives • Writing a friendly letter • Changing *y* to *i* to add *-es, -ed* • Forming plural possessive of nouns • Reflexive pronouns • Plurals with *-es* • Irregular verbs • Journal writing	• Predicting • Summarizing • Fact and opinion • Comparing and contrasting • Sequence • Inference • Making judgments • Drawing conclusions • Classifying	• Reading help wanted ads • Payment schedule • Reading a map • Telephone safety • Reading ads • Filling out a form • Reading a menu
• Using adjectives • Writing names and titles • Writing complete sentences • Recognizing fragments • Past tense of verbs • Pronouns • Recognizing run-ons • Journal writing	• Predicting • Summarizing • Recalling facts • Character traits • Main idea • Cause and effect • Inference • Sequence • Drawing conclusions • Writer's tone and purpose • Fact and opinion	• Finding library materials • Registering to vote • Writing a summary of qualifications • Completing a medical form • Filling out a credit application • Being a good listener • Reading abbreviations

DISCUSSION

Remember
Look at the picture. Have you ever been to a music store like this?

Predict
Look at the picture and the story title. What do you think this story is about?

Instructor's Notes: Read the discussion questions to students. Discuss the story title, the characters, and the situation in the picture.

A Plan To Save the Store

My brother Max has a music store. He likes the work and the people who stop in. Max loves guitars. His friends say he is good at fixing old guitars. I'd like to have a job I can love like Max loves his.

At one time the money Max got from the music store was good. But times are not the same. People do stop by the store, but they don't buy like they did. Max is in big trouble. Is it time for him to quit? Or can I help Max make a plan to save the store? If I can help him, he can help me get a job.

Instructor's Notes: Have students read silently or read together. Have students underline words they don't recognize. Review the underlined words. Have students identify the speaker.

Review Words

A. Check the words you know.

- ☐ 1. plan
- ☐ 2. goods
- ☐ 3. guitars
- ☐ 4. quit
- ☐ 5. lose
- ☐ 6. old
- ☐ 7. music
- ☐ 8. won't
- ☐ 9. some
- ☐ 10. time
- ☐ 11. help
- ☐ 12. trouble

B. Read and write the sentences. Circle all the review words.

1. Max has trouble with his music store.

_____

2. Some of the goods in the store are old.

_____

3. Max likes to fix old guitars.

_____

4. Max won't quit, but it's time for him to get some help.

_____

_____

5. Will Max find a plan, or will he lose money?

_____

C. Write a sentence. Use a review word.

_____

_____

_____

Instructor's Notes: Read each set of directions to students. For A, have students read the words aloud and then check known words. In B, explain the meaning of *goods* in this context: "wares" or "merchandise."

Sight Words

see
tapes
sell

A. Read the words in color. Then read the sentence.

I see that Max has no music tapes to sell.

B. Underline the new words in sentences 1-4.

1. When people stop by the store, they don't see tapes for sale.

2. Max can sell tapes in his music store.

3. He can make bigger sales with tapes.

4. Will Max see that tapes can help the store?

C. Write the three new words into the puzzle.

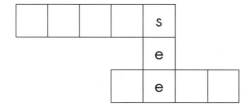

D. Write the word that completes each sentence.

sell   tape   see

1. Goods that are out of date don't _____ .

2. People like to buy music on _____ .

3. Will Max _____ that my plan will make money?

E. Write your own sentence. Use one of the new words.

_____

_____

Instructor's Notes: Read each set of directions to students. Read each sight word aloud. Have students repeat. Discuss the difference between the words *sell* and *sale*.

Sight Words

take
records
shop

Note: The letters s and h go together to stand for the sh sound in the word shop.

A. Read the words in color. Then read the sentence.

Take the records out of the shop.

B. Underline the new words in sentences 1–4.

1. Max has a lot of old records in the shop.

2. We can sell the records for a quarter.

3. I'll help out in Max's shop from time to time.

4. It will take time to make the shop look good.

C. Look down and across. Find the words in the box. Circle them.

shop

take

records

h	r	e	c	o	r	d	s
s	v	t	b	d	l	g	h
u	y	t	a	k	e	f	o
a	j	i	q	t	m	z	p

D. Write the word that completes each sentence.

record   take   shop

1. Max will keep a _____ of the store's sales.

2. People can't _____ for tapes in Max's Music Store.

3. I see that it will _____ a lot of work to save the store.

E. Write your own sentence. Use one of the new words.

_____

Instructor's Notes: Read each set of directions to students. Read each sight word aloud. Have students repeat. Read the *sh* note in the box. Ask students for other examples of words that begin with *sh*. Tell students that *shop* can be used as a noun or a verb. In C, point out another meaning for *record*: "facts that are written down."

Sight Words

video
down
value

A. Read the words in color. Then read the sentence.

Will this video go down in value?

B. Underline the new words in sentences I–4.

1. Sales are down in Max's store.

2. I'll talk to him about the value of selling videos.

3. He can both rent and sell videos at the shop.

4. Max will see the value in this plan.

C. Write the letters in the order that makes a word.

lvuae _____value_____

wond _____

evodi _____

D. Write the word that completes each sentence.

    value   videos   down

1. When we go _____ to the shop, Max and I find lots of people.

2. They can see our store has a lot of _____ for sale.

3. Max sees the _____ in selling tapes and videos.

E. Write your own sentence. Use one of the new words.

_____

_____

Instructor's Notes: Read each set of directions to students. Encourage students to practice writing sentences from Review Word and Sight Word pages in a notebook or journal. Have students practice changing statements to questions.

Phonics: Short e

-ell

sell
fell
tell
well
shell

A. Read the words in color. Write other -ell words.

b + ell = <u>bell</u>

D + ell = _____

N + ell = _____

y + ell = _____

B. Read the sentences. Circle the words with -ell. Write them.

1. Max's music shop was not doing (well). <u>well</u>

2. Can you see why the store fell on bad times? _____

3. What is Max going to sell in his store? _____

4. Tell some friends to stop by the store. _____

C. Write your own sentence. Use an -ell word.

_____

_____

D. Look across. Find the new words. Mark out letters that do not belong in each new word.

1. ☒ | Y | E | L | L | ☒ | ☒

2. P | Z | W | E | L | L | J

3. A | M | U | B | E | L | L

4. K | F | E | L | L | S | X

Instructor's Notes: Show students the -ell word pattern in the known sight word *sell*. Then read each set of directions to students. For A, tell students that the words have the short e vowel sound. Review the *sh* sound in *shell*.

Phonics: Long a

-ake
take
fake
make
sake
shake

A. Read the words in color. Write other _-ake_ words.

b + ake = _____

l + ake = _____

r + ake = _____

w + ake = _____

B. Read the sentences. Circle the words with _-ake_.
Write them.

1. Max did take a good look at his shop. _____

2. He can make money selling videos. _____

3. Max had to wake up to what people are buying.

   _____

4. I am helping out for Max's sake. _____

C. Write your own sentence. Use an _-ake_ word.

_____

_____

D. Circle the right word in each sentence.

1. Max will find a plan to (make, bake) money.

2. He will do it for the (take, sake) of his family.

3. Max will (shake, take) a chance on renting videos.

4. Video stores can (rake, lake) in the money.

Instructor's Notes: Show students the _-ake_ word pattern in the known sight word _take_. Then read each set of directions to students. For A, tell students that the words have the long _a_ vowel sound. Remind students that when words in the _cvc + e_ pattern end in a silent e, the preceding vowel sound is usually long.

video + tape = videotape

A. Read the words. Write the new words.

1. up + set = <u>upset</u>

2. some + times = _____

3. down + hill = _____

4. work + out = _____

5. out + let = _____

B. Read the compound words. Write the word that fits best in each sentence.

downhill   upset   workout   videotapes   sometimes

Max is _____ about the music store. Sales are

going _____ . Max loves the store, but

_____ he feels like quitting.

I tell Max to rent _____ . People who

like to keep fit will use the _____ tapes. Max

will have to take a chance to save the store.

C. Draw lines to match the two words that make a compound word.

1. home   stand
2. eye   one
3. pan   glasses
4. band   sick
5. some   cake

Instructor's Notes: Read the example together. Explain that compound words are two words that combine to form a word with a new meaning. Read each set of directions to students.

BACK TO THE STORY

■■■■■■■■■ **Remember**

What has happened in the story so far?

■■■■■■■■■ **Predict**

Look at the picture. What do you think will happen in the rest of the story?

A Plan To Save the Store

Kent: Look at all the videos, tapes, and CDs you have! Max, how did you get the money for all of this?

Max: I came up with a sales plan and talked to some friends. It was a good plan, and they lent me the money. I had to take a chance, Kent.

Kent: It was time to take a chance. Records are going down in value. People like to buy music on tapes.

Max: I see that, Kent. And with all these tapes, videos, and CDs, how can I lose?

Instructor's Notes: Read the questions to students. Help students review and predict. Read the story aloud to students or have them read silently. Tell students that CDs are compact discs.

15

At the end of the day, Max sits down at his desk. He makes a record of the store's sales. This job takes time, but keeping good records is the key to running a shop that makes money. Max has to keep up with what people like.

Sales are bigger in Max's store. He sells a lot of tapes and CDs. People like pop, big band, rap, and country music. Videotape sales are bigger than music sales in Max's shop. Max keeps tapes for people of all ages. He has videos like The Jetsons for children and ones like Batman for all the family. Max finds that a lot of people like workout videos. When people buy workout videos, they have fun and get fit.

Instructor's Notes: Read both pages to students or have them read silently.

Kent: Well, big brother, it looks like the plan to save Max's Music Store worked. Look at all the people, the videos, and the tapes. How about that!

Max: I got lucky, Kent. But it wasn't all luck. It was a brother like you who helped me see the value in a good plan. Some friends with the money helped me take a big chance.

Kent: I can see how you've worked. I'll bet you feel good.

Max: It feels good to pay back the friends who lent me money. I feel good that I didn't quit.

Kent: Do you still find time to work on the old guitars? A lot of people say you are tops at fixing them.

Max: Yes, but doing a good job takes a lot of time. To keep up with my work on the guitars, I'll have to get someone to help out in the shop. Say, Kent, how about working with me in the store?

Kent: Well, I didn't plan on this. But you don't have to sell me. How can we lose with a good plan, a lot of work, and good luck?

Comprehension

Think About It
1. Why was Max's store losing money?
2. How did he change the store?
3. When did the store start to make money?
4. Sum up what happened in the story.

Write About It
What do you think is the key to success in running a business?

Instructor's Notes: Help students read and answer the questions. **Write About It** can be used as a writing or discussion assignment. Use the Unit 1 Review on page 90 to conclude the unit. Then assign *Reading for Today Workbook Three*, Unit 1.

DISCUSSION

Remember
Look at the picture. What can a photo album tell about your past?

Predict
Look at the picture and the story title. What do you think the story is about?

Instructor's Notes: Read the discussion questions to students. Discuss the story title, the woman, and the situation in the picture.

Looking Out for Me

I've had a lot of mothers and fathers. My brother Ed and I went from home to home. We had some good times and some bad times. Some of the people did love children and helped us. Some people didn't like us at all. At my age I can look at all this and laugh, but I feel I have lots of troubles to work out.

Instructor's Notes: Have students read silently or read together. Have students underline words they don't recognize. Review the underlined words. Have students identify the speaker.

Review Words

A. Check the words you know.

☐ 1. age   ☐ 2. brother   ☐ 3. children

☐ 4. father   ☐ 5. feel   ☐ 6. find

☐ 7. from   ☐ 8. laugh   ☐ 9. lucky

☐ 10. mother ☐ 11. them   ☐ 12. went

B. Read and write the sentences. Circle the review words.

1. My brother and I went from home to home.

_____

2. Some children end up in a bad home.

_____

3. I feel like Nell and Bill are my mother and father.

_____

_____

4. They had time to talk and laugh with us.

_____

5. At this age I can see that I was lucky to find them.

_____

_____

C. Write a sentence. Use a review word.

_____

_____

Instructor's Notes: Read each set of directions to students. For A, have students read the words aloud and then check known words.

Sight Words

parents
who
give

A. Read the words in color. Then read the sentence.

Some children have good <u>parents</u> <u>who</u> <u>give</u> them love.

B. Underline the new words in sentences 1–4.

1. Some people don't have children, but they can be parents.

2. They are people who have love to give.

3. They take in children who don't have parents.

4. They give the children food, love, and a good home.

C. Look down and across. Find the words in the box. Circle them.

give

parents

who

b	f	u	g	w	h	o
k	e	w	i	m	j	q
h	o	c	v	r	l	d
p	a	r	e	n	t	s

D. Write the word that completes each sentence.

give   who   parents

1. The Lins are people _____ don't have children.

2. They feel that they can be good _____ .

3. The Lins can _____ a lot of love to children.

E. Write your own sentence. Use one of the new words.

_____

Instructor's Notes: Read each set of directions to students. Read each sight word aloud. Have students repeat.

Sight Words

own
fine
life

A. Read the words in color. Then read the sentence.

My <u>own</u> parents didn't have a <u>fine</u> <u>life</u>.

B. Underline the new words in sentences 1–4.

1. My father was in fine health, but he got sick.

2. Mother had a lot of trouble in her life.

3. Her own parents didn't love her.

4. Mother's life wasn't good, but she didn't give up.

C. Write the three new words into the puzzle.

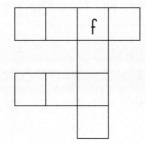

D. Write the word that completes each sentence.

own   life   fine

1. Ed and I had a chance for a good _____.

2. We had a _____ home with Bill and Nell Lin.

3. It was sad that our _____ parents didn't help us.

E. Write your own sentence. Use one of the new words.

_____

_____

Instructor's Notes: Read each set of directions to students. Read each sight word aloud. Have students repeat.

Sight Words

hug
social worker
when

Note: The letters w and h go together to stand for the wh sound in the word when.

A. Read the words in color. Then read the sentence.

We got a hug from the social worker when we got to our home.

B. Underline the new words in sentences 1-4.

1. When my father got sick, he had to give up his job.

2. The social worker had to find us a home.

3. Dad gave Ed and me a big hug when we went.

4. The social worker helped us find Bill and Nell.

C. Write the letters in the order that makes a word.

guh _____

lciosa krowre _____ _____

henw _____

D. Write the word that completes each sentence.

    hugs   when   social worker

1. Our _____ _____ helped us find a good family.

2. Kids get upset _____ they feel no one loves them.

3. A lot of _____ can make a kid feel good.

E. Write your own sentence. Use one of the new words.

_____

Instructor's Notes: Read each set of directions to students. Read each sight word aloud. Have students repeat. Read the *wh* note in the box. Ask for other words that begin with *wh*.

23

Phonics: Short u

−ug

hug

bug

dug

rug

A. Read the words in color. Write other −ug words.

j + ug = _____

l + ug = _____

m + ug = _____

t + ug = _____

B. Read the sentences. Circle the words with −ug. Write them.

1. We got a jug of water to take with us to the lake.

   _____

2. We have an old rug to sit down on. _____

3. I bet the bugs will bite us. _____

4. The car dug a hole in the wet sand. _____

C. Write your own sentence. Use a −ug word.

_____

_____

D. Look across. Find the new words. Mark out letters that do not belong in each new word.

1. | Q | L | U | G | K |

2. | T | U | G | K | X |

3. | V | B | C | U | G |

4. | G | H | U | G | H |

Instructor's Notes: Show students the -ug word pattern in the known sight word *hug*. Then read each set of directions to students. For A, tell students that a single vowel in a word ending in a consonant often stands for the short vowel sound.

Phonics: Long i

-ine
fine
line
nine
wine
shine

A. Read the words in color. Write other -ine words.

d + ine = _____

m + ine = _____

p + ine = _____

v + ine = _____

wh + ine = _____

B. Read the sentences. Circle the words with -ine.
Write them.

1. When I was nine, Nell let me get a dog. _____

2. We had a fine time playing games. _____

3. All dogs whine from time to time. _____

4. Owners have to learn to keep a dog in line.

_____

C. Write your own sentence. Use an -ine word.

_____

_____

D. Circle the right word in each sentence.

1. Don't (vine, shine) the light in my eyes.

2. A friend of (mine, pine) is working with children.

3. The family will (dine, line) at seven.

4. The old table is made of (shine, pine).

Instructor's Notes: Show students the *-ine* word pattern in the known sight word *fine*. Then read each set of directions to students. For A, remind students that the *-ine* word family fits the *cvc + e* pattern. Vowels that follow this pattern are usually long.

Language: Irregular Plurals

child
children

A. Some words do not add –s to mean more than one. Read the words. Write the words that mean more than one.

One	More Than One	
woman	women	_____
life	lives	_____
leaf	leaves	_____
this	these	_____
man	men	_____
person	people	_____

B. Practice reading the sentences.

Ed and I have had some troubles in our lives. We are lucky that the social worker helped us. People who had love to give became our parents. These men and women gave us good homes.

Sometimes children who can't find good parents give up on life. With help from people who love them, these kids can see that they are fine people.

C. Write one of these words in each sentence.

children   men   Women

1. _____ like Nell make good mothers.

2. Some women can't have _____ .

3. When _____ become fathers, they learn a lot about children.

Instructor's Notes: Read each set of directions to students. Discuss the example. Explain that some words form plurals by changing letters in the words, not by adding -s. After students read B, ask them to circle the irregular plurals.

BACK TO THE STORY

■■■■■■■■■ **Remember**
What has happened in the story so far?
■■■■■■■■■ **Predict**
Look at the picture. What job does the young woman have? How do you think her life will turn out?

Looking Out for Me

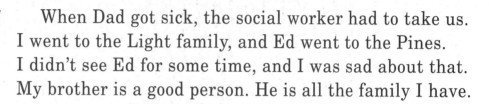

When Dad got sick, the social worker had to take us. I went to the Light family, and Ed went to the Pines. I didn't see Ed for some time, and I was sad about that. My brother is a good person. He is all the family I have.

But time is going on. I'm a woman of 18. When I got to be this age, I went out on my own. The social worker helped me get a job at the lake. I like the water, and I like to work with children. I'm doing a lot with my life.

Instructor's Notes: Read the questions to students. Help students review and predict. Read the story aloud to students or have them read silently.

For the time being, I have a home with a friend of mine. We get by, but I won't stop at this. With work and luck, I can have children of my own. I can make a good home for my family.

You can bet I'll be a good mother! I'll give my children all my love. I'll see that my kids eat well. I won't yell at them when they make mistakes. I'll see that my children have a father who is a fine man.

If my children have troubles, we will learn to talk it out. A family who can learn to talk about troubles will do fine.

Instructor's Notes: Read both pages to students or have them read silently.

When I was a child, I had a chance to learn the value of a good family. I met some fine men and women. When I have my own family, I'll be a good parent like Nell and Bill Lin. The Lins helped me see that having good parents gives a child a chance to do well in life.

Sometimes I tend to feel sad like my mother did. When life gets me down, I find a friend to talk with. Sometimes a big hug is all it takes. I won't let my chances go by. My life is my own, and I'll make it a good one.

Comprehension

Think About It

1. What kind of childhood did the girl and her brother have?
2. Who helped the children most? Why do you think so?
3. What did the girl learn from her experiences with the families she lived with?
4. Sum up what happened in the story.

Write About It

Do you think the young woman in this story is unusual? Explain why or why not.

Instructor's Notes: Help students read and answer the questions. **Write About It** can be used as a writing or discussion assignment. Use the Unit 2 Review on page 91 to conclude the unit. Then assign *Reading for Today Workbook Three*, Unit 2.

29

DISCUSSION

Remember
Look at the picture. Where does the story take place? Have you ever been to a place like this?

Predict
Look at the picture and the story title. What do you think this story is about?

Instructor's Notes: Read the discussion questions to students. Discuss the story title, the characters, and the situation in the picture.

In Good Health

My job is helping people who are sick. I see people of all ages. When people are in bad health, I work to help make them well.

I work with nurses and with social workers. The nurses talk to parents about family health. The social workers talk to people who have troubles or feel sad when they walk in.

Chances are that we can't win all the time, but we do our job.

Instructor's Notes: Have students read silently or read together. Have students underline words they don't recognize. Review the underlined words. Have students identify the speaker.

Review Words

A. Check the words you know.

- [ ] 1. about
- [ ] 2. but
- [ ] 3. chance
- [ ] 4. fine
- [ ] 5. glasses
- [ ] 6. group
- [ ] 7. health
- [ ] 8. nurse
- [ ] 9. smoke
- [ ] 10. smoking
- [ ] 11. social worker
- [ ] 12. talk

B. Read and write the sentences. Circle the review words.

1. When a mother smokes, she takes a chance with her child's health.

   _____

2. Our social worker can get glasses for people who don't have money.

   _____

   _____

3. A nurse talks to groups about family health.

   _____

4. When I eat well, I feel fine.

   _____

5. I have to quit smoking, but I can't give it up.

   _____

C. Write a sentence. Use a review word.

_____

_____

Sight Words

clinic
hope
doctor

Note: The letters c and l go together to stand for the cl sound in the word clinic.

A. Read the words in color. Then read the sentence.

People who go to a clinic hope the doctor can help them.

B. Underline the new words in sentences 1-3.

1. At a good clinic, all who walk in get help.

2. People hope the doctor can tell them what to do.

3. At the clinic, the doctor helps people get well.

C. Write the three new words into the puzzle.

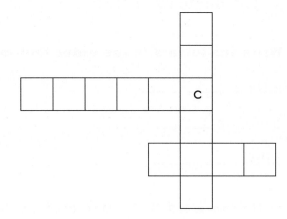

D. Write the word that completes each sentence.

hopes   doctor   clinic

1. Dan went to see the _____ about his smoking.

2. The doctor sent Dan to a group at the _____ .

3. Dan _____ to quit smoking with the group's help.

E. Write your own sentence. Use one of the new words.

_____

Instructor's Notes: Read each set of directions to students. Read each sight word aloud. Have students repeat. Read the *cl* note in the box. Ask for other words that begin with *cl*.

Sight Words

what
problem
said

Note: The letters <u>p</u> and <u>r</u> go together to stand for the <u>pr</u> sound in the word <u>problem</u>.

A. Read the words in color. Then read the sentences.

<u>What</u> <u>problem</u> do you have?

The nurse <u>said</u> she can help.

B. Underline the new words in sentences 1–4.

1. The woman said her hand wasn't mending.

2. What can she do about this problem?

3. The nurse can tell the woman what to do.

4. The nurse can help her work on the problem.

C. Write the letters in the order that makes a word.

adis _____

brelmop _____

tahw _____

D. Write the word that completes each sentence.

problems   said   what

1. Doctors at the clinic see lots of _____ .

2. The doctors tell people _____ to do to get well.

3. The nurse _____ the clinic gives people hope.

E. Write your own sentence. Use one of the new words.

_____

_____

Instructor's Notes: Read each set of directions to students. Read each sight word aloud. Have students repeat. Read the *pr* note in the box. Ask for other words that begin with *pr*.

Sight Words

want
more
hip

A. Read the words in color. Then read the sentence.

I <u>want</u> <u>more</u> help for my bad <u>hip</u>.

B. Underline the new words in sentences 1–4.

1. Nan wants to see the doctor about her hip.

2. Standing and sitting makes her hip feel bad.

3. The doctor wants Nan to walk more.

4. He said more walking is good for her hip.

C. Look down and across. Find the words in the box. Circle them.

want

more

hip

r	m	c	g	e	v	w
z	o	w	a	n	t	b
s	r	d	h	i	p	l
k	e	f	y	u	w	q
c	h	j	k	e	b	x

D. Write the word that completes each sentence.

want   more   hip

1. I have trouble with my _____ .

2. I _____ to do what the doctor said.

3. I don't want _____ health problems.

E. Write your own sentence. Use one of the new words.

_____

Instructor's Notes: Read each set of directions to students. Read each sight word aloud. Have students repeat.

Phonics: Short i

–ip
hip
lip
sip
tip
clip
ship

A. Read the words in color. Write other –ip words.

d + ip = _____

n + ip = _____

r + ip = _____

z + ip = _____

B. Read the sentences. Circle the words with –ip. Write them.

1. The nurse has lots of health tips. _____

2. When the child fell down, he cut his lip. _____

3. A sip of cold water will help. _____

C. Write your own sentence. Use an –ip word.

_____

_____

D. Look across. Find the new words. Mark out letters that do not belong in each new word.

1. | T | N | I | P | V |

2. | E | C | L | I | P |

3. | T | M | R | I | P |

4. | S | H | I | P | Z |

5. | G | A | Z | I | P |

36 **Instructor's Notes:** Show students the *-ip* word pattern in the known sight word *hip*. Then read each set of directions to students. For A, tell students that the *i* in *hip* stands for the short vowel sound. Review the *cl* sound in *clip*.

Phonics: Long o

-ope
hope
cope
rope

A. Read the words in color. Write other -ope words.

l + ope = _____

m + ope = _____

p + ope = _____

B. Read the sentences. Circle the words with -ope. Write them.

1. Jan feels that she has no hope of getting well.

   _____

2. She sits in bed and mopes about her problems.

   _____

3. Jan can't cope with bad health. _____

4. I hope that Jan will get well. _____

C. Write your own sentence. Use an -ope word.

_____

_____

D. Circle the right word in each sentence.

1. We all have to (cope, lope) with health problems from time to time.

2. It's my job to make the beds, but I can (mope, rope) Ned into helping me.

Instructor's Notes: Show students the -ope word pattern in the known sight word *hope.* Then read each set of directions to students. For A, remind students that the -ope word family fits the *cvc + e* pattern. Vowels that follow this pattern are usually long.

Language: Adding –er to Words

work + er = worker

A. Add –er. Write the new words.

1. buy + er = _____

2. help + er = _____

3. read + er = _____

4. smoke + er = _____

5. talk + er = _____

6. play + er = _____

B. Practice reading the sentences.

Ned Cutman is a man who was a smoker. When he quit, he wanted to be a helper at the health clinic. Sometimes he helps with the children. Ned is a good reader. He makes the children laugh.

Ned is a big talker. This makes people feel OK when they have to sit for a time in the clinic.

C. Write the word that fits best in each sentence.

helper   talker   reader   smoker

1. Ned Cutman is a man who was a _____ .

2. He wanted to be a _____ at the clinic.

3. Ned is a good _____ .

4. Ned is a big _____ .

Instructor's Notes: Read each set of directions to students. Discuss the example. Explain that adding -er to verbs changes them to nouns. The -er ending changes the verb to mean "one who does the action." After students read B, ask them to circle the -er words.

BACK TO THE STORY
■■■■■■■■■ **Remember**
What has happened in the story so far?
■■■■■■■■■ **Predict**
Look at the picture. What do you think will happen in the rest of the story?

At the Clinic

Daily Log

8:00 A.M.	Pat R., age 8 Problem: A dog nipped Pat's hand. I talked to Pat, to her father, and to the dog's owner. He said that the dog is in good health. Pat will be fine. Her hand looks OK.
8:30 A.M.	Jake B., age 32 Problem: Jake can't cope with his family's problems. I sent him to the clinic social worker. He tells me that Jake and his family want to go into a group for some help.
9:00 A.M.	Jed P., age 19 Problem: Jed has trouble when he eats the wrong foods. I want him to stop eating dips, nuts, and cake. Jed said he will do what I want. I'll send him to a doctor who can help us find out more about the foods that are bad for him.

Instructor's Notes: Read the questions to students. Help students review and predict. Explain that the Daily Log is a record of the doctor's appointments with patients. Read the story aloud to students or have them read silently.

Daily Log

9:15 A.M.	Van A., age 63
	Problem: Van smokes, but at his age, he feels that he can't stop. In time he will have more and more problems. I want him to go to the clinic's stop-smoking group. Without this group, I don't have a lot of hope for this smoker.
9:45 A.M.	Lin H., age 52
	Problem: Lin feels down and out. Her health is good, but she sits at home all the time. She mopes about her life. She has to get out and see people. This will give her a chance to make friends. I'll talk to the social worker about this.
10:30 A.M.	Dot S., age 2
	Problem: Dot has a big red cut on her lip. It looks like someone hit her. She won't eat. I went to see Dot's parents, but they won't talk about it. Her home life isn't good. The social worker said I have to make a record of these problems.

Instructor's Notes: Read both pages to students or have them read silently.

Daily Log

11:00 A.M.	Kip R., age 73 Problem: A man will be in with his father. The father fell down at the store and landed on his hip. I'll see him, but I have some more people to see by sundown.
1:00 P.M.	A social worker from the clinic wants me to talk to a group of children about the food they eat. They want me to tell them about good health.
4:00 P.M.	I've got some records to read. I hope I can get to this. I don't like to take work home.
7:00 P.M.	It's good that we love what we do at the clinic. Our work has no end to it. In time, we'll win the love of the people who use our clinic.

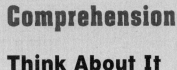

Comprehension

Think About It

1. What are the doctor's main responsibilities?
2. How does the doctor keep track of daily problems?
3. Do you think the doctor has a good method of keeping patient records? Why or why not?
4. Sum up what happened in the story.

Write About It

How do you think the doctor feels about her job?

Instructor's Notes: Help students read and answer the questions. **Write About It** can be used as a writing or discussion assignment. Use the Unit 3 Review on page 92 to conclude the unit. Then assign *Reading for Today Workbook Three*, Unit 3.

DISCUSSION

Remember

Look at the picture. What do you think is happening? What experiences have you had playing a team sport?

Predict

Look at the picture and the story title. What do you think this story is about?

Instructor's Notes: Read the discussion questions to students. Discuss the story title, the characters, and the situation in the picture.

A Chance To Play

When my friends and I get out of work, we go to the lot. We all love to play, and all nine men are good players. We have fun winning, but we can laugh when we lose.

The trouble is that Jan, a woman we work with, wants to play with us. We like her OK on the job, but we don't want her to be a player. The boss said we have to give her a chance. I have a feeling that this is the end of our good times!

Instructor's Notes: Have students read silently or read together. Have students underline words they don't recognize. Review the underlined words. Have students identify the speaker.

Review Words

A. Check the words you know.

☐ 1. all   ☐ 2. boss   ☐ 3. friends

☐ 4. fun   ☐ 5. got   ☐ 6. lot

☐ 7. love   ☐ 8. lucky   ☐ 9. nine

☐ 10. our   ☐ 11. out   ☐ 12. play

B. Read and write the sentences. Circle the review words.

1. All our friends stop by the lot to see the fun.

   _____

   _____

2. All nine of us love to get out and play.

   _____

3. We get lucky sometimes and win.

   _____

4. We have fun when we play.

   _____

5. Our boss got the lot for the nine of us to use.

   _____

   _____

C. Write a sentence. Use a review word.

   _____

   _____

Instructor's Notes: Read each set of directions to students. For A, have students read the words aloud and then check known words.

Sight Words

need
baseball
team

A. Read the words in color. Then read the sentence.

Do we <u>need</u> a woman on our <u>baseball</u> <u>team</u>?

B. Underline the new words in sentences 1–4.

1. Someone said that Jan is good at baseball.

2. Our team needs nine top players to win.

3. Has Jan played baseball on a men's team?

4. The boss said that Jan will need our help.

C. Write the letters in the order that makes a word.

ened _____

aemt _____

sealblab _____

D. Write the word that completes each sentence.

baseball   team   need

1. The men on the _____ don't want Jan to play.

2. We're lucky we have a team that loves

   _____.

3. Jan will _____ friends to give her some tips.

E. Write your own sentence. Use one of the new words.

_____

_____

Instructor's Notes: Read each set of directions to students. Read each sight word aloud. Have students repeat. Explain that *baseball* is a compound word. Students will see the words *base* and *ball* used separately throughout Unit 4.

Sight Words

day
does
game

A. Read the words in color. Then read the sentence.

<u>Day</u> by <u>day</u> we see that Jan <u>does</u> play the <u>game</u> well.

B. Underline the new words in sentences 1–4.

1. We're going to the game to see Jan play.

2. It does look like she will be a good player.

3. She will get to be tops at this game one day.

4. Maybe our team does need her help.

C. Look down and across. Find the words in the box. Circle them.

day

game

does

e	h	p	d	a	y	j
q	w	u	o	z	v	l
p	l	q	e	p	i	d
r	z	d	s	k	b	c
m	g	a	m	e	j	h

D. Write the word that completes each sentence.

does   day   game

1. Jan _____ a good job of hitting the ball.

2. We have stopped laughing at her _____ .

3. One _____ Jan is going to help our team win.

E. Write your own sentence. Use one of the new words.

Instructor's Notes: Read each set of directions to students. Read each sight word aloud. Have students repeat.

Sight Words

because
there
uniform

Note: The letters t and h go together to stand for the th sound in the words there, that, them, they, and the.

A. Read the words in color. Then read the sentence.

Jan got mad <u>because</u> <u>there</u> was no <u>uniform</u> for her.

B. Underline the new words in sentences 1–3.

1. There was going to be a big game at the lot.

2. Jan had to mend the rips in an old uniform.

3. Jan was feeling fine because she played well.

C. Write the three new words into the puzzle.

D. Write the word that completes each sentence.

because   uniform   there

1. A big group of people from work was _____.

2. We yelled _____ we wanted to win.

3. Jan went to bat in her mended _____.

E. Write your own sentence. Use one of the new words.

_____

Instructor's Notes: Read each set of directions to students. Read each sight word aloud. Have students repeat. Read the *th* note in the box. Ask for other words that begin with *th*.

Phonics: Long a

-ay
day
may
pay
way
clay
play

A. Read the words in color. Write other -ay words.

h + ay = _____

J + ay = _____

l + ay = _____

r + ay = _____

s + ay = _____

B. Read the sentences. Circle the words with -ay. Write them.

1. This may be our lucky day. _____ _____

2. Lay down the bat and run, Ray! _____ _____

3. That's the way to play this game! _____ _____

C. Write your own sentence. Use an -ay word.

_____

_____

D. Look across. Find the new words. Mark out letters that do not belong in each new word.

1. Q H A Y X E

2. R T P A Y U

3. A C Z S A Y

4. J A Y L I W

5. T C L A Y F

Instructor's Notes: Show students the -ay word pattern in the known sight word *day*. Then read each set of directions to students. For A, tell students that -ay stands for the long *a* vowel sound.

Phonics: Long e

-eed
need
deed
feed
heed

A. Read the words in color. Write other –eed words.

r + eed = _____

s + eed = _____

w + eed = _____

B. Read the sentences. Circle the words with –eed.
Write them.

1. The players need to have some fun. _____

2. I can feed the baseball team at my home.

    _____

3. That will be my good deed for the team. _____

C. Write your own sentence. Use an –eed word.

_____

_____

D. Circle the right word in each sentence.

1. Someone has to cut the (seeds, weeds) on the lot.

2. The players (need, deed) uniforms for the game.

3. It takes a lot of money to (reed, feed) a baseball team.

4. (Heed, Feed) my words: Play to win!

Instructor's Notes: Show students the –eed word pattern in *need*. Then read the directions to students.
For A, tell students that –ee stands for the long e vowel sound. Explain that when two vowels are side by side, the
first vowel is usually long and the second is silent. Examples include the –ee in *need* and the –ea in *team*.

Language: Recognizing Sentences

A sentence begins with a capital letter.
A telling sentence ends with a period ⬚.
An asking sentence ends with a question mark ⬚?
A strong feeling ends with an exclamation mark ⬚!

Examples: It's our big day!
Will we win the game?
We have a good chance.

A. Read the sentences. Then write them below.

1. The Lake City team didn't have a woman player.

2. Did they want Jan?

3. You bet they did!

_____

_____

_____

_____

B. Write a telling sentence, an asking sentence, and a sentence with strong feeling.

1. _____

2. _____

_____

3. _____

_____

Instructor's Notes: Read the rules together. Discuss the examples. Read each set of directions to students. Remind students that sentences begin with a capital letter and end with a period, a question mark, or an exclamation mark.

BACK TO THE STORY

■ ■ ■ ■ ■ ■ ■ ■ ■ **Remember**

What has happened in the story so far?

■ ■ ■ ■ ■ ■ ■ ■ ■ ■ **Predict**

Look at the picture. What do you think will happen in the rest of the story?

A Chance To Play

◢ Ray: That was some game! Did you see the way Jake hit the ball?

Ann: Yes, and did you see Jan's winning run?

Ray: Jan played well, and so did you and Kay. We're lucky to have the three of you on our team today. With three men out sick, we had a big problem.

Ann: Jan, Kay, and I have wanted to play on the team for some time. I hope you can see that women can play baseball well.

Ray: OK, there are some good women players. I see that, but not all women are good at baseball.

Ann: Well, not all men are good players. Some of the women have talked about getting our own baseball team going. That way we can play with a group of people who want us.

Instructor's Notes: Read the questions to students. Help students review and predict. Point out that the names at the left show who is speaking in the story. Read the story aloud to students or have them read silently. Help students pronounce the proper name *Ann*, pointing out that it is pronounced like *an*.

[The men have a talk...]

Ted: What about our team? We need good players, and the boss said we have to give the women a chance to play.

Ray: The boss can tell a good baseball player when he sees one! Did you see Ann run the bases? And Kay got four hits.

Jake: These women love baseball, and they're fun to have on the team. But what's this about an all-women's group? If they get a women's team going, they won't want to play with us. What can we do to stop them?

Ted: Let's talk to them and see what they say. We have to make the women see that we want them on our team because they're good players, not because they're women.

Ray: I hope they'll go for it. With them I bet we can set a record.

Instructor's Notes: Read both pages to students or have them read silently. Explain that the dialogues on pages 51, 52, and 53 are three separate conversations that all take place following the game.

[The men and women players work it out...]

Ted: What do you say, Jan? Will you play on the men's baseball team? What about Kay and Ann?

Jan: So you want us on the team? It's about time! Women can be good baseball players, but we can do well with a team of our own.

Jake: Don't say that! We need you on our baseball team.

Kay: What's in it for us? Will we get good uniforms that fit? Will we get to play a lot?

Ann: We'll want some say in the way the team is run. That's the way it has to be.

Ray: OK, OK . . . the team needs you women. You win!

Jan: No, Ray. It's time for you to see that we all win!

Comprehension

Think About It

1. How did the three women get a chance to play on the men's team?
2. Why did the women want to form their own team?
3. When did the men decide that women should be on their team?
4. Sum up what happened in the story.

Write About It

Why do men and women sometimes have trouble working together?

Instructor's Notes: Help students read and answer the questions. **Write About It** can be used as a writing or discussion assignment. Use the Unit 4 Review on page 93 to conclude the unit. Then assign *Reading for Today Workbook Three*, Unit 4.

DISCUSSION

Remember

Look at the picture. What experiences have you had training or teaching an animal?

Predict

Look at the picture and the story title. What do you think this story is about?

Instructor's Notes: Read the discussion questions to students. Discuss the story title, the characters, and the situation in the picture.

Helping Dogs To Help People

When I got in trouble with the cops, I had the feeling that my life was at an end. Today I see that life wasn't ending for me. I got into a group that works with dogs. We send the dogs out to people who need them.

Today I work with Sundown, a big, fine dog. I feed him and see that he has all the water he needs. When he does well, he gets a big hug from me.

The key to working with dogs is love. It's good to have this job because it gives me hope for my own life.

Instructor's Notes: Have students read silently or read together. Have students underline words they don't recognize. Review the underlined words. Have students identify the speaker.

Review Words

A. Check the words you know.

- [ ] 1. be
- [ ] 2. did
- [ ] 3. do
- [ ] 4. does
- [ ] 5. dog
- [ ] 6. eat
- [ ] 7. eyes
- [ ] 8. fed
- [ ] 9. his
- [ ] 10. mistake
- [ ] 11. my
- [ ] 12. send

B. Read and write the sentences. Circle the review words.

1. My dog wants to do well, but sometimes he makes mistakes.

_____

2. His eyes shine with pride when he does well.

_____

3. Sundown likes to eat, and he will be fed two times a day.

_____

_____

4. Did Sundown eat all his food?

_____

5. I send my dog out to play when his work ends.

_____

C. Write a sentence. Use a review word.

_____

_____

Instructor's Notes: Read each set of directions to students. For A, have students read the words aloud and then check known words.

Sight Words

prison
learn
teach

Note: The letters p and r go together to stand for the pr sound in the words prison and problem.

A. Read the words in color. Then read the sentence.

In prison we learn to teach dogs.

B. Underline the words in sentences 1-4.

1. Not all prisons give people a chance like this.

2. The dogs we teach will help people someday.

3. The dogs learn to work with people who need them.

4. I hope I can use this prison job when I get out.

C. Write the three new words into the puzzle.

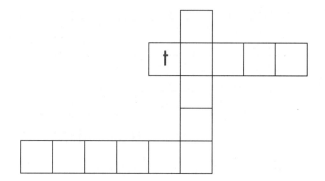

D. Write the word that completes each sentence.

learning   prison   teach

1. Prison can _____ me to cope with life.

2. I'm _____ to use my time well.

3. I can't say that _____ is a lot of fun.

E. Write your own sentence. Use one of the new words.

_____

Instructor's Notes: Read each set of directions to students. Read each sight word aloud. Have students repeat. Read the *pr* note in the box. Ask for other words that begin with *pr*.

Sight Words

disabled
different
things

Note: The letters t and h go together to stand for the th sound in there. But th can also stand for the whispered th sound in thing and thin.

A. Read the words in color. Then read the sentence.

A disabled person can use a dog for different things.

B. Underline the new words in sentences 1-4.

1. We teach our dogs to do different things.

2. These dogs are helpers for disabled people.

3. People have different needs for our dogs.

4. Dogs help disabled people to get out.

C. Write the letters in the order that makes a word.

leddabis _____

gtnihs _____

fentfirde _____

D. Write the word that completes each sentence.

disabled   different   things

1. I am learning _____ ways to do

_____ with my dog's help.

2. My dog has helped me see that being _____ is OK.

E. Write your own sentence. Use one of the new words.

_____

_____

Sight Words

June
come
right

A. Read the words in color. Then read the sentence.

June said that the dog will come right to her.

B. Underline the new words in sentences 1-4.

1. June had to learn to work with her dog.

2. She learned the right way to tell the dog what to do.

3. The dog comes when June calls it.

4. June has the right dog for her needs.

C. Look down and across. Find the words in the box. Circle them.

come

June

right

s	w	d	a	l	c	n
f	l	p	c	k	o	y
r	i	g	h	t	m	b
a	k	j	u	n	e	x
z	q	b	f	p	d	v

D. Write the word that completes each sentence.

June   right   come

1. Working with dogs is _____ for me.

2. It makes me feel good to help _____ .

3. The time will _____ when June will go home.

E. Write your own sentence. Use one of the new words.

_____

Instructor's Notes: Read each set of directions to students. Read each sight word aloud. Have students repeat.

Phonics: Long i

-ight
right
fight
night
sight

A. Read the words in color. Write other –ight words.

l + ight = _____

m + ight = _____

t + ight = _____

B. Read the sentences. Circle the words with –ight. Write them.

1. Our dogs help people with bad sight. _____

2. They are on the job day and night. _____

3. Disabled people need to find a dog that is right for them. _____

C. Write your own sentence. Use an –ight word.

_____

_____

D. Look across. Find the new words. Mark out letters that do not belong in each new word.

1. G F I G H T L

2. B C M I G H T

3. L I G H T J Z

4. E T I G H T A

5. D P N I G H T

Instructor's Notes: Show students the *-ight* word pattern in the known sight word *right*. Then read each set of directions to students. For A, tell students that *-igh* often spells the long *i* vowel sound. The letters *g* and *h* are silent.

Phonics: Long u

−une and −ute
June
dune
tune
prune

A. Read the words in color. Write –ute words below.

c + ute = _____

l + ute = _____

m + ute = _____

B. Read the sentences. Circle the words with –une and –ute. Write them.

1. Some disabled people can't talk. They are mute.

_____

2. June has trouble getting about in the city because she can't see. _____

3. Her dog may be cute, but it isn't a pet. _____

C. Write your own sentence. Use a –une or –ute word.

_____

_____

D. Circle the right word in each sentence.

1. I want to learn that (tune, dune) on the radio.

2. The children played in the sand (dunes, prunes).

3. I learned to talk with my hands because I am (lute, mute).

4. My dog can do (cute, mute) things.

Instructor's Notes: Show students the *-une* word pattern in the known sight word *June*. Introduce the *-ute* word pattern. Then read each set of directions to students. For A, remind students that the *-une* and *-ute* word families fit the *cvc + e* pattern. Vowels that follow this pattern are usually long.

work - worked   do - did

We add –ed to some words to show the past.
Other words change the spelling to show the past.

A. Write the words that show the past time.

Present Time	Past Time		Present Time	Past Time	
come	came	_____	go	went	_____
say	said	_____	take	took	_____
is	was	_____	give	gave	_____
are	were	_____	feed	fed	_____

B. Practice reading the sentences.

I came to this prison to do time. Some of the prisoners were working with dogs. One day I went to see them. They gave me a dog to work with. Working with Sundown took a lot of time, but helping out gave me a good feeling.

C. Write one of these words in each sentence.

gave   was   were   did

1. I _____ not have a job. I _____ in need of work.

2. Some of the prisoners _____ working with dogs.

3. They _____ me a dog to work with.

Instructor's Notes: Read each set of directions to students. Discuss the examples. Explain that some verbs form the past tense by changing letters in the words, not by adding -ed. These words are called irregular verbs because they don't follow a regular pattern.

BACK TO THE STORY

■■■■■■■■ **Remember**

What has happened in the story so far?

■■■■■■■■ **Predict**

Look at the picture. What do you think will happen in the rest of the story?

Helping Dogs To Help People

To June,

I hope you and Sundown are doing fine. He is a good dog and learned all the right things to help you. Sometimes I'm sad because he had to go. But Sundown isn't a pet—he's a working dog with a job to do.

These days I'm working with a different dog. Zip is a cute dog who likes to eat. He has a lot to learn, but I've got lots of time to teach him.

This job is helping me see that I've got something to give. Disabled people who want to use a dog might need my help. Teaching dogs to help people is a good thing for a woman in prison to learn.

Can you and Sundown come to see me? I send both of you my love.

Fay

Instructor's Notes: Read the questions to students. Help students review and predict. Point out that the rest of the story is in the form of letters. Ask students who writes and who receives the letter on this page. Read the story aloud to students or have them read silently.

63

To Fay,

Sundown and I are doing fine. We're learning different ways of getting about in the city. He walks me to the clinic and to see friends. My boss said I can take Sundown on the job. You were right. With Sundown's help, I can be on my own.

Sundown might not get homesick for the prison, but he does get homesick for you. You were his teacher. You fed him and gave him a lot of love.

When I came to the prison, I was about to give up. Today things are different. It took time, but I learned to do a lot of things without my sight. People who become disabled don't need to feel that life has ended.

June

To June,

Today I learned that I might get out of prison in May! What will I do? Maybe I can get a job helping disabled people. The social worker said she will help me find a job.

In the old days, I made a lot of mistakes. I ended up in prison. But when I get out, I will have a different life.

When I came to prison, it took some time to see that there was hope for my life. But today I feel I can make it on my own without getting in more trouble.

I'll come to see you and Sundown when I get out.

Fay

Comprehension

Think About It

1. What skill did Fay learn while she was in prison?
2. How do you think Fay feels about the dogs she trains?
3. When did June find her life getting better?
4. Sum up what happened in the story.

Write About It

What kind of work makes you feel most useful? Why?

Instructor's Notes: Help students read and answer the questions. **Write About It** can be used as a writing or discussion assignment. Use the Unit 5 Review on page 94 to conclude the unit. Then assign *Reading for Today Workbook Three*, Unit 5.

DISCUSSION

Remember

Look at the picture. What do you think is happening? What do you know about the day-to-day lives of truckers?

Predict

Look at the picture and the story title. What do you think this story is about?

Instructor's Notes: Read the discussion questions to students. Discuss the story title and the picture.

A Life on the Go

I'm on the go all the time. Sometimes I'm in the country, and sometimes I'm in a city. I'm on my own a lot of the time.

I want to have more time with my family—more time with Hope and my children, Mike and Pam. There are lots of holidays when I can't be at home with them.

I bet that a lot of people feel the way I do. But a job is a job, and this is the work I'm fit to do. Being on the go all the time is my way of life.

Instructor's Notes: Have students read silently or read together. Have students underline words they don't recognize. Review the underlined words. Have students identify the speaker.

Review Words

A. Check the words you know.

- ☐ 1. ads
- ☐ 2. bet
- ☐ 3. bigger
- ☐ 4. fit
- ☐ 5. hand
- ☐ 6. holiday
- ☐ 7. no
- ☐ 8. on
- ☐ 9. read
- ☐ 10. son
- ☐ 11. upset
- ☐ 12. will

B. Read and write the sentences. Circle the review words.

1. I bet I won't make it home on the holidays.

   _____

2. My son will be upset about that.

   _____

3. I bet a job with a bigger store will fit my needs.

   _____

4. I read the ads, but there are no jobs for someone like me.

   _____

5. Maybe my friend Bill will give me a hand.

   _____

C. Write a sentence. Use a review word.

_____

_____

 Instructor's Notes: Read each set of directions to students. For A, have students read the words aloud and then check known words.

Sight Words

drive
rig
road

Note: The letters d and r go together to stand for the dr sound in the word drive.

A. Read the words in color. Then read the sentence.

I drive my rig down the road.

B. Underline the new words in sentences 1-4.

1. In my job I'm on the road day and night.

2. When I drive my rig, I have my C.B. radio on all the time.

3. I talk to people like me who are on the road.

4. I'm lucky to own the rig I drive.

C. Write the letters in the order that makes a word.

igr _____

aodr _____

viedr _____

D. Write the word that completes each sentence.

    drive   road   rig

1. There are no stores on this country _____.

2. I'll have to _____ into the city to get food.

3. I worked for some time to buy my own _____.

E. Write your own sentence. Use one of the new words.

_____

_____

Instructor's Notes: Read each set of directions to students. Read each sight word aloud. Have students repeat. Read the *dr* note in the box. Ask for other words that begin with *dr*. Explain that the word *rig* is another word for *truck*. Explain that C.B. radios are used by truckers for short–distance conversations.

Sight Words

truck
heavy
carry

Note: The letters t and r go together to stand for the tr sound in truck and trouble.

A. Read the words in color. Then read the sentence.

My truck is heavy and can carry a lot.

B. Underline the new words in sentences 1–4.

1. The more I carry, the more money I can make.

2. This time my truck will carry heavy goods.

3. When I carry heavy goods, I need more time to get there.

4. It's a big job to drive a heavy truck.

C. Look down and across. Find the words in the box. Circle them.

truck

heavy

carry

q	j	t	r	u	c	k
z	g	p	l	i	a	f
v	f	d	y	l	r	m
x	k	q	l	s	r	x
l	h	e	a	v	y	z

D. Write the word that completes each sentence.

carry   heavy   truck

1. My old friend Bill drives a _____ like mine.

2. Our rigs are fitted for _____ goods.

3. There are a lot of laws about what goods a rig can

_____ .

E. Write your own sentence. Use one of the new words.

Instructor's Notes: Read each set of directions to students. Read each sight word aloud. Have students repeat. Read the tr note in the box. Ask for other words that begin with tr.

Sight Words

cold
lonely
mind

A. Read the words in color. Then read the sentence.

When I drive on a <u>cold</u>, <u>lonely</u> road, I have a lot on my <u>mind</u>.

B. Underline the new words in sentences 1–4.

1. On cold days like this, I get lonely.

2. On good days, I don't mind being on the road.

3. It's a lonely job to drive a heavy rig all day.

4. Hope and the children are on my mind.

C. Write the three new words into the puzzle.

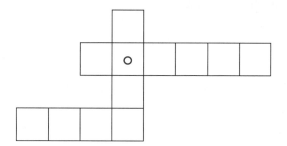

D. Write the word that completes each sentence.

cold   lonely   mind

1. My _____ is with my family.

2. When it's _____ out, I want to be home.

3. Feeling _____ comes with the job.

E. Write your own sentence. Use one of the new words.

_____

Instructor's Notes: Read each set of directions to students. Read each sight word aloud. Have students repeat. Point out two meanings of *mind*: "thoughts" and "to dislike."

Phonics: Short i

-ig
rig
big
dig

A. Read the words in color. Write other -ig words.

f + ig = _____

p + ig = _____

w + ig = _____

B. Read the sentences. Circle the words with -ig. Write them.

1. Some truckers carry pigs in from the country.

   _____

2. Can I learn to drive a heavy rig? _____

3. My son wants to drive a truck when he gets big.

   _____

C. Write your own sentence. Use an -ig word.

_____

_____

D. Look across. Find the new words. Mark out letters that do not belong in each new word.

1. K R I G D

2. L X W I G

3. P I G Q L

4. Y D I G Z

Instructor's Notes: Show students the -ig word pattern in the known sight word rig. Then read each set of directions to students. For A, tell students that the i stands for its short sound in these words.

Phonics: Long o

-old
cold
fold
old
sold

A. Read the words in color. Write other –old words.

b + old = _____

g + old = _____

h + old = _____

m + old = _____

t + old = _____

B. Read the sentences. Circle the words with –old. Write them.

1. It's cold and lonely on the road. _____

2. I'll hold on to the job because it pays well.

_____

3. I hope the rig won't be sold. _____

C. Write your own sentence. Use an –old word.

_____

_____

D. Circle the right word in each sentence.

1. The truck I drive is red and (gold, hold).

2. The truck is set up to carry (bold, cold) foods.

3. The boss (fold, told) me to drive at night.

4. He (sold, gold) the food on the truck to a food store.

Instructor's Notes: Show students the –old word pattern in the known sight word cold. Then read each set of directions to students. For A, tell students that the letter o stands for the long vowel sound in these words. Note that these words do not end in silent e.

Language: Dropping Final –e To Add –ed and –ing

hope + ed = hoped   hope + ing = hoping

Some words like *hope* end in –e.
To add –ed or –ing to a word, drop the –e.

A. Drop the letter –e. Add –ed. Then add –ing.

1. fake   _____   _____

2. like   _____   _____

3. love   _____   _____

4. time   _____   _____

5. tune   _____   _____

6. use   _____   _____

B. Practice reading the sentences.

I loved trucks and cars when I was a child. I liked to be with my dad, and sometimes I used to drive with him to work. He had a job tuning up cars and vans. I learned from Dad about a car's timing. Today I'm a trucker, and I've used what I learned from Dad.

C. Write one of these words in each sentence.

tuning   loved   timing

1. I _____ trucks and cars when I was a child.

2. Dad had a job _____ up cars and vans.

3. I learned about a car's _____ from him.

Instructor's Notes: Read the rules together. Discuss the examples. Read each set of directions to students. Discuss how the different tenses of the verbs are used.

BACK TO THE STORY

▪▪▪▪▪▪▪▪▪ **Remember**

What has happened in the story so far?

▪▪▪▪▪▪▪▪▪ **Predict**

Look at the picture. What do you think will happen in the rest of the story?

A Life on the Go

Hope: It will feel good to give you a big hug when you get home, Dell. I get lonely for you, and I need help with the kids. Mike has a cold. Pam fell down and got a bad cut on her leg. I had to take her to the clinic. Can't you quit this trucking job and find work at home?

Dell: It's no fun having a job on the road, Hope. You and Mike and Pam are on my mind all the time. But people who drive heavy rigs make good money. I've told you that.

Instructor's Notes: Read the questions to students. Help students review and predict. Point out that the names at the left show who is speaking in the story. Read the story aloud to students or have them read silently. Invite students to take the parts of the different characters and read the story aloud.

75

Mike: Hi, Dad! Things are OK, but I've got some problems. I got in a fight today because some kid said I was fat. Pam wants to play with me all the time, but I end up having to carry her. She gets heavy! When you come home, will you read to me about trucks?

Dell: I love reading to you, son. But don't tell me you want to drive a rig like I do. It gets cold and lonely on the road. Sometimes I don't get home in time for the holidays.

Hope: You can tell that Mike loves his dad! Mike told me he wants to have his own rig when he's bigger. But can my son cope with the life of a trucker?

Instructor's Notes: Read both pages to students or have them read silently. Explain that Hope is thinking to herself in the last paragraph and not speaking aloud.

Hope: The time you have at home does go by!

Dell: Being on the road all the time gets old. When the kids get bigger, maybe my sister will keep them from time to time. She's a lot of fun, and they like her. Then I can take you with me on the road. I love you, Hope. Having you with me will keep me from being lonely.

Hope: I wanted you to say that, Dell. It makes me feel good. I love you, and driving the rig will give us lots of time to talk. There is a big country out there to see. Down the road, there will be lots of love and no more lonely times.

Comprehension

Think About It

1. Why does Dell keep in touch with his family?
2. What problems does Hope have to handle on her own?
3. How does Dell feel about his job? How do his wife and family feel about his job?
4. Sum up what happened in the story.

Write About It

Would you like "a life on the go"? Why or why not?

Instructor's Notes: Help students read and answer the questions. **Write About It** can be used as a writing or discussion assignment. Use the Unit 6 Review on page 95 to conclude the unit. Then assign *Reading for Today Workbook Three*, Unit 6.

77

DISCUSSION

Remember

Look at the picture. Have you ever seen a vacant lot like this?

Predict

Look at the picture and the story title. What do you think the story is about?

Instructor's Notes: Read the discussion questions to students. Discuss the story title, the woman, and the situation in the picture.

Together We Stand

When I was a child, I used to play on this lot. It was safe, and we had a lot of fun. Today the lot is run down. Look at all the weeds and the glass. Children can get hurt playing in the lot.

Parents say they are sick of this problem, but no one does a thing about it. It's time someone did! Maybe that someone is me.

Instructor's Notes: Have students read the page silently or together. Have students underline words they don't recognize. Review the underlined words. Have students identify the speaker. Show students how the words *glass* and *safe* are part of the known sight words *glasses* and *safety*.

Review Words

A. Check the words you know.

☐ 1. about	☐ 2. children	☐ 3. hope
☐ 4. hurt	☐ 5. parents	☐ 6. person
☐ 7. play	☐ 8. right	☐ 9. safety
☐ 10. see	☐ 11. there	☐ 12. want

B. Read and write the sentences. Circle the review words.

1. Parents are upset about the safety of the children who play in this lot.

   _____

   _____

2. Can you see all the glass and weeds there?

   _____

3. It's not right to let children play where they might get hurt.

   _____

   _____

4. I hope someone can do something about the problem.

   _____

5. I want to be the person who helps.

   _____

C. Write a sentence. Use a review word.

   _____

Instructor's Notes: Read each set of directions to students. For A, have students read the words aloud and then check known words.

Sight Words

camera
still
photo

Note: The letters s and t go together to stand for the st sound in the words still, stop, and store.

A. Read the words in color. Then read the sentence.

Hold the camera still when you take a photo.

B. Underline the new words in sentences 1–4.

1. You need a good camera to take good photos.

2. I used to take a lot of photos of my children.

3. Getting children to sit still for a photo is a problem.

4. My children are older, but I still take a lot of photos.

C. Look down and across. Find the words in the box. Circle them.

camera

photo

still

v	o	t	j	m	i	c	s
b	s	g	x	q	i	l	t
q	c	a	m	e	r	a	i
n	p	h	o	t	o	i	l
p	k	f	d	v	z	a	l

D. Write the word that completes each sentence.

camera   still   photos

1. Where did you set the _____ you were using?

2. You set it down when you stopped taking _____ .

3. I bet Nell _____ has the camera.

E. Write your own sentence. Use one of the new words.

_____

Instructor's Notes: Read each set of directions to students. Read each sight word aloud. Have students repeat. Explain that the *ph* in photo sounds like *f*. For B, point out two meanings of *still*: "without motion" and "continue to." Read the *st* note. Ask for other words that begin with *st*.

Sight Words

street

drag

action

Note: The letters s, t, and r go together to stand for the str sound in the word street.

A. Read the words in color. Then read the sentence.

Will these photos of the <u>street</u> <u>drag</u> some <u>action</u> out of the city?

B. Underline the new words in sentences 1–3.

1. This street sees a lot of action.

2. The lot at the end of the street is a big problem.

3. We want action, but the talking drags on and on.

C. Write the three new words into the puzzle.

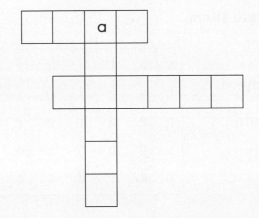

D. Write the word that completes each sentence.

action   drag   street

1. People with homes on this _____ are upset.

2. The kids use the street to have _____ races.

3. The home owners want the city to take _____ .

E. Write your own sentence. Use one of the new words.

---

82 **Instructor's Notes:** Read each set of directions to students. Read each sight word aloud. Have students repeat. In D, point out another meaning of *drag*: "a type of car race." Read the *str* note in the box. Ask for other words that begin with *str*.

Sight Words

many
together
beat

A. Read the words in color. Then read the sentence.

When <u>many</u> people work <u>together</u>, they can <u>beat</u> a big problem.

B. Underline the new words in sentences 1–4.

1. Many parents are upset about the safety of the children.

2. No one can beat a group of parents who are upset.

3. Together they can make the city do something.

4. When parents stand together, they can beat a problem.

C. Write the letters in the order that makes a word.

ateb _____

getherto _____

yamn _____

D. Write the word that completes each sentence.

many   beat   together

1. When I was a kid, I played _____ baseball games on this lot.

2. My team used to spend all day _____.

3. No one can _____ you when you play as a team.

E. Write your own sentence. Use one of the new words.

_____

Instructor's Notes: Read each set of directions to students. Read each sight word aloud. Have students repeat.

83

Phonics: Short a

-ag

drag

bag

rag

sag

A. Read the words in color. Write other -ag words.

g + ag = _____

l + ag = _____

n + ag = _____

t + ag = _____

w + ag = _____

B. Read the sentences. Circle the words with -ag.
Write them.

I. Rosa has to carry a heavy camera bag. _____

2. She drags it with her all the time. _____

3. Sometimes Rosa lags behind us to take a photo. _____

4. Don't nag Rosa if she takes a lot of photos. _____

C. Write your own sentence. Use an -ag word.

_____

_____

D. Look across. Find the new words. Mark out letters that
do not belong in each new word.

I. Q T A G K

2. G A G K U

3. O V W A G

4. L R A G H

Instructor's Notes: Show students the -ag word pattern in the known sight word *drag.* Then read each
set of directions to students. For A, tell students that the words have the short *a* vowel sound. Review the
dr sound in *drag.*

Phonics: Long e

–eat
beat
heat
neat
treat

A. Read the words in color. Write other –eat words.

f + eat = _____

s + eat = _____

m + eat = _____

wh + eat = _____

B. Read the sentences. Circle the words with –eat. Write them.

1. The lot has to be safe and neat. _____

2. Do you feel the city will treat us right? _____

3. City Hall can seat many people. _____

4. Together we can make the city feel the heat.

_____

C. Write your own sentence. Use an –eat word.

_____

_____

D. Circle the right word in each sentence.

1. The weeds in the lot are as tall as (meat, wheat).

2. The sun (treats, beats) down on us all day.

3. The (heat, seat) can make you feel sick.

4. With a bit of work, we can make the lot look (feat, neat).

Instructor's Notes: Show students the –*eat* word pattern in the known sight word *beat*. Then read each set of directions to students. For A, tell students that the words have the long *e* vowel sound. Review the rule about vowels appearing in a word side by side. Review the *tr* sound in *treat* and the *wh* sound in *wheat*.

85

Language: Writing Quotations

Rules

1. Put quotation marks (" ") before and after what a person says to show the words spoken.
2. Put a comma (,) between these quoted words and the rest of the sentence.
3. The first word the person says begins with a capital letter.

Examples: "Come see the photos," Will said.

"The photos are in the *City Sun*," said Rosa.

A. Practice reading the sentences.

"Getting the city to take action on that lot makes me feel good," said Rosa. "I hope people see that together we can beat this problem."

Will said, "I want the city to take a look at my street. Many trucks use the street. The trucks are there day and night. Children aren't safe to play on the street."

B. Write each sentence below. Write in quotation marks, commas, and capital letters.

1. will said can i help you carry that heavy camera?

_____

_____

2. it isn't heavy to me said rosa.

_____

3. let me use the camera to take a photo said will.

_____

Instructor's Notes: Read the rules together. Discuss the examples. Read each set of directions to students. Encourage students to read the conversation aloud to show the expression of the speakers.

BACK TO THE STORY

■■■■■■■■■ **Remember**

What has happened in the story so far?

■■■■■■■■■■ **Predict**

Look at the picture. What do you think will happen in the rest of the story?

Together We Stand

"What are you doing with that camera?" said Will.

"I'm taking photos of this run-down lot," I said. "The weeds need to be cut. And look at all the glass!"

"That's the way things are," said Will.

"Maybe," I said. "But I've got to do something. I'll send the photos to the *City Sun*. The *Sun* can use my photos to make the city see the problem."

"Well, give it a shot," said Will, "but it may not work. Rosa," he said, "this problem is bigger than one person. Get together with the people on this street. You need them to back you up. One person can't do it all."

Instructor's Notes: Read the questions to students. Help students review and predict. Read the story aloud to students or have them read silently. Review the use of quotation marks for conversation. Help the student pronounce the proper name *Rosa*. Explain that the *City Sun* is a newspaper.

Things were humming on Clay Street. People were talking about the photo in the *City Sun*.

"Good going, Rosa!" they said. "Maybe this will shake things up at City Hall. Did the *Sun* pay you for your photo?"

"Yes indeed," I said. "I hope I can get more work with the *Sun*."

"You did a good job with that camera, but we still don't see the city taking action," said Will. "Sometimes problems like this drag on and on. The city might not have the money to pay for the work we need."

About that time three city trucks came down the street. They stopped at the lot. Workers got out and set to work.

Will's eyes lit up, and he let out a big laugh.

"Rosa, you were right not to give up. Together with that camera, you have helped people on Clay Street get the help they needed."

Instructor's Notes: Read both pages to students or have them read silently. Explain to the student that the photo in the newspaper is Rosa's published work.

The workers came back to the lot on Clay Street many times. A family or two stopped by and stayed to help. More and more people came by to help. By the time the lot was fixed, the people of Clay Street had learned to work together.

I took a lot of photos of the group. I wanted to use my camera to help people see teamwork in action. If I'm lucky, maybe the *City Sun* will use my photos one more time.

Today the lot on Clay Street is neat and safe. At sundown the kids get together to play baseball. Parents drop by to see who will win. We take a lot of pride in the work we did on the lot.

I still have my home on Clay Street. Today my friends and I are working to get a health clinic. The people who have homes on Clay have learned a lot. We've learned that one person can't do it all. We've learned to stand together.

Comprehension

Think About It

1. Why did Rosa first take photos of the lot?
2. What did Rosa learn from her experience with the vacant lot?
3. Have you ever tried to do something about a problem in your neighborhood?
4. Sum up what happened in the story.

Write About It

Did someone ever try to discourage you from working to solve a problem? What did you do or say?

Instructor's Notes: Help students read and answer the questions. **Write About It** can be used as a writing or discussion assignment. Use the Unit 7 Review on page 96 to conclude the unit. Then assign *Reading for Today Workbook Three*, Unit 7.

A. Complete each sentence. Use each word only once.

tapes	see	sells
shop	take	records
video	value	down

1. The store _____ guitars and _____ .

2. People like to buy music on _____ .

3. Sales are _____ in the store.

4. The _____ of the shop may go down.

B. Write –ell or –ake to make new words. Write the word that fits best in each sentence.

1. s + _____ = _____   I _____ records in my store.

2. w + _____ = _____   Records don't sell as _____ as they did.

3. t + _____ = _____   It will _____ a good plan to save the store.

4. m + _____ = _____   My brother will help me _____ a plan.

C. Read each sentence. Find the compound word and write it.

1. Sometimes my brother plays a guitar. _____

2. I am upset about the store. _____

3. Sales in my shop are going downhill. _____

4. Workout videos sell well. _____

5. People like to rent videotapes. _____

Unit 2 Review

A. Complete each sentence. Use each word only once.

fine	hug	social worker
give	own	parents
life	who	when

1. Some children have _____ who _____ them love.

2. My _____ parents didn't have a fine _____ .

3. The _____ _____ helped us find a home.

4. I'll _____ my children _____ I have my own.

B. Write –ug or –ine to make new words. Write the word that fits best in each sentence.

1. h + _____ = _____   I got a _____ from Bill.

2. r + _____ = _____   I got water on the _____ .

3. f + _____ = _____   I had a _____ life with Nell.

4. n + _____ = _____   I was _____ when I got a dog.

C. Write the word that fits best in each sentence.

1. One _____ loved us.
   <u>woman, women</u>

2. All of her _____ played with us.
   <u>child, children</u>

3. _____ children liked us.
   <u>This, These</u>

4. All the _____ in the family helped us.
   <u>man, men</u>

Unit 3 Review

A. Complete each sentence. Use each word only once.

clinic	said	want
doctor	what	more
problem	hope	hip

1. The _____ at the _____ helps people.

2. The doctor _____ she can help me with my _____.

3. I _____ I can get _____ help.

4. I _____ my _____ to mend.

B. Write –ip or –ope to make new words. Write the word that fits best in each sentence.

1. h + _____ = _____   The man fell and landed on his _____.

2. t + _____ = _____   The nurse can give me a _____.

3. h + _____ = _____   Jan can't give up _____ of getting well.

4. c + _____ = _____   She will _____ with the problem.

C. Write the words that end in –er.

1. Ned wanted to be a helper at the clinic. _____

2. He helped a player with a cut lip. _____

3. Ned is a good worker at the clinic. _____

4. He helped a smoker to stop smoking. _____

5. The children said Ned is a good reader. _____

A. Complete each sentence. Use each word only once.

team	day	baseball
need	does	because
game	there	uniform

1. We _____ Jan on our _____ _____ .

2. Jan will be tops at the _____ one _____ .

3. She _____ well _____ she works at it.

4. _____ will be a good _____ for Jan.

B. Write –ay or –eed to make new words. Write the word that fits best in each sentence.

1. n + _____ = _____   The players _____ to win a game.

2. f + _____ = _____   Will you _____ the dog?

3. s + _____ = _____   I _____ we will win.

4. m + _____ = _____   We _____ win with Jan.

C. Write the sentence. Add a [?], [!], or [.].

1. Jan ran to the base _____

2. Will she make it home _____

3. What a hit _____

4. Did they win _____

5. No way _____

6. Can women play baseball as well as men _____

_____

Unit 5 Review

A. Complete each sentence. Use each word only once.

teach	right	different
learn	June	disabled
thing	come	prison

1. In _____ we _____ to _____ dogs.

2. I teach the dogs to _____ _____ to me.

3. The dogs help _____ people get about in the city.

4. People have _____ needs for our dogs.

B. Write –ight or –une to make new words. Write the word that fits best in each sentence.

1. m + _____ = _____   A disabled person _____ need a dog.

2. s + _____ = _____   June has learned to do things without her _____.

3. f + _____ = _____   Dogs have to learn not to _____ .

4. J + _____ = _____   _____ uses a dog to help her.

C. Draw lines to match the present tense of the word with the past tense.

1. come   did
2. do   were
3. is   went
4. are   came
5. go   gave
6. give   was

Unit 6 Review

A. Complete each sentence. Use each word only once.

> rig   mind   lonely
> road   truck   drive
> cold   heavy   carry

1. I _____ my _____ down the _____ .

2. My _____ is _____ and can _____ a lot.

3. I can get _____ and _____ on the road.

4. I have a lot on my _____ .

B. Write –ig or –old to make new words. Write the word that fits best in each sentence.

1. r + ____ = _____   I drive a heavy _____.

2. b + ____ = _____   I need a _____ truck.

3. c + ____ = _____   It's _____ and lonely sometimes.

4. s + ____ = _____   The rig will not be _____.

C. Add –ed and –ing to the words. Write the correct words on the lines below.

1. like   _____   _____

2. love   _____   _____

3. smoke   _____   _____

4. tape   _____   _____

5. time   _____   _____

6. use   _____   _____

A. Complete each sentence. Use each word only once.

photos	camera	still
drag	action	street
beat	many	together

1. My _____ is in the heavy bag.

2. _____ people want the city to take _____ .

3. The children play _____ in the _____ .

4. I _____ take a lot of _____ .

B. Write –ag or –eat to make new words. Write the word that fits best in each sentence.

1. b + _____ = _____   I carry a heavy camera _____ .

2. t + _____ = _____   The children play _____ in the street.

3. h + _____ = _____   Can the city feel the _____?

4. b + _____ = _____   Nothing can _____ a good photo.

C. Write each sentence, adding quotation marks, commas, and capital letters.

1. i can help you with that heavy bag said will.

_____

2. Rosa said it's not as heavy as it looks.

_____

3. i can see you are good at taking photos said will.

_____

Answer Key

● ● ● ● ●

Unit 1

▶ **Page 8**

A. Answers will vary.

B. 1. Max has ⟨trouble⟩ with his ⟨music⟩ store.
2. ⟨Some⟩ of the ⟨goods⟩ in the store are ⟨old⟩.
3. Max likes to fix ⟨old⟩ ⟨guitars⟩.
4. Max ⟨won't⟩ ⟨quit⟩, but it's ⟨time⟩ for him to get ⟨some⟩ ⟨help⟩.
5. Will Max find a ⟨plan⟩, or will he ⟨lose⟩ money?

C. Discuss your sentence with your instructor.

▶ **Page 9**

B. 1. When people stop by the store, they don't <u>see</u> <u>tapes</u> for sale.
2. Max can <u>sell</u> <u>tapes</u> in his music store.
3. He can make bigger sales with <u>tapes</u>.
4. Will Max <u>see</u> that <u>tapes</u> can help the store?

C.

t	a	p	e	s	
				e	
	s	e	l	l	

D. 1. sell
2. tape
3. see

E. Discuss your sentence with your instructor.

▶ **Page 10**

B. 1. Max has a lot of old <u>records</u> in the <u>shop</u>.
2. We can sell the <u>records</u> for a quarter.
3. I'll help out in Max's <u>shop</u> from time to time.
4. It will <u>take</u> time to make the <u>shop</u> look good.

C.
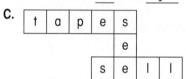

D. 1. record
2. shop
3. take

E. Discuss your sentence with your instructor.

▶ **Page 11**

B. 1. Sales are <u>down</u> in Max's store.
2. I'll talk to him about the <u>value</u> of selling <u>videos</u>.
3. He can both rent and sell <u>videos</u> at the shop.
4. Max will see the <u>value</u> in this plan.

C. value, down, video

D. 1. down
2. videos
3. value

E. Discuss your sentence with your instructor.

▶ **Page 12**

A. bell, Dell, Nell, yell

B. 1. Max's music shop was not doing ⟨well⟩.
2. Can you see why the store ⟨fell⟩ on bad times?
3. What is Max going to ⟨sell⟩ in his store?
4. ⟨Tell⟩ some friends to stop by the store.

C. Discuss your sentence with your instructor.

D. 1. X̶ Y E L L G̶ H̶
2. P̶ Z̶ W E L L X̶
3. X̶ M U̶ B E L L
4. K F E L L S̶ X̶

▶ **Page 13**

A. bake, lake, rake, wake

B. 1. Max did ⟨take⟩ a good look at his shop.
2. He can ⟨make⟩ money selling videos.
3. Max had to ⟨wake⟩ up to what people are buying.
4. I am helping out for Max's ⟨sake⟩.

C. Discuss your sentence with your instructor.

D. 1. make
   2. sake
   3. take
   4. rake

▶ **Page 14**

A. 1. upset
   2. sometimes
   3. downhill
   4. workout
   5. outlet

B. upset, downhill, sometimes, videotapes, workout

C.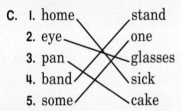
   1. home — glasses
   2. eye — cake
   3. pan — stand
   4. band — one
   5. some — sick

▶ **Page 17**

Think About It

Discuss your answers with your instructor.

1. Max didn't have up-to-date products in his store.
2. He began to sell videos, CDs and tapes.
3. The store began to make money when customers rented and bought the new tapes, CDs and videos.
4. Summaries should include the idea that Max did not want to change his store at first. Later, with his brother's help and friends' money, he did change his store and it became a healthy business again.

Write About It

Discuss your writing with your instructor.

Unit 2

▶ **Page 20**

A. Answers will vary.

B. 1. My ⟨brother⟩ and I ⟨went⟩ ⟨from⟩ home to home.
   2. Some ⟨children⟩ end up in a bad home.
   3. I ⟨feel⟩ like Nell and Bill are my ⟨mother⟩ and ⟨father⟩.
   4. They had time to talk and ⟨laugh⟩ with us.
   5. At this ⟨age⟩ I can see that I was ⟨lucky⟩ to ⟨find⟩ ⟨them⟩.

C. Discuss your sentence with your instructor.

▶ **Page 21**

B. 1. Some people don't have children, but they can be <u>parents</u>.
   2. They are people <u>who</u> have love to give.
   3. They take in children <u>who</u> don't have parents.
   4. They <u>give</u> the children food, love, and a good home.

C.
b	f	u	g	w	h	o
k	e	w	i	m	j	q
h	o	c	v	r	l	d
p	a	r	e	n	t	s

D. 1. who
   2. parents
   3. give

E. Discuss your sentence with your instructor.

▶ **Page 22**

B. 1. My father was in <u>fine</u> health, but he got sick.
   2. Mother had a lot of trouble in her <u>life</u>.
   3. Her <u>own</u> parents didn't love her.
   4. Mother's <u>life</u> wasn't good, but she didn't give up.

C.

l	i	f	e
		i	
o	w	n	
		e	

D. 1. life

2. fine

3. own

E. Discuss your sentence with your instructor.

▶ **Page 23**

B. 1. <u>When</u> my father got sick, he had to give up his job.

2. The <u>social</u> <u>worker</u> had to find us a home.

3. Dad gave Ed and me a big <u>hug</u> <u>when</u> we went.

4. The <u>social</u> <u>worker</u> helped us find Bill and Nell.

C. hug, social worker, when

D. 1. social worker

2. when

3. hugs

E. Discuss your sentence with your instructor.

▶ **Page 24**

A. jug, lug, mug, tug

B. 1. We got a (jug) of water to take with us to the lake.

2. We have an old (rug) to sit down on.

3. I bet the (bugs) will bite us.

4. The car (dug) a hole in the wet sand.

C. Discuss your sentence with your instructor.

D. 1. ⟨Ø⟩ L U G ⟨X⟩

2. T U G ⟨K⟩ ⟨X⟩

3. ⟨Y⟩ B ⟨C⟩ U G

4. ⟨G⟩ H U G ⟨X⟩

▶ **Page 25**

A. dine, mine, pine, vine, whine

B. 1. When I was (nine), Nell let me get a dog.

2. We had a (fine) time playing games.

3. All dogs (whine) from time to time.

4. Owners have to learn to keep a dog in (line).

C. Discuss your sentence with your instructor.

D. 1. shine

2. mine

3. dine

4. pine

▶ **Page 26**

A. women, lives, leaves, these, men, people

C. 1. Women

2. children

3. men

▶ **Page 29**

<u>Think About It</u>

Discuss your answers with your instructor.

1. They didn't have parents and lived in many different homes.

2. Answers will vary.

3. She learned the value of a good family and that having good parents gives a child a chance to do well in life.

4. Summaries should include the idea that the girl had a rough childhood, had a set of loving foster parents, and had the determination to succeed on her own.

<u>Write About It</u>

Discuss your writing with your instructor.

Unit 3

▶ **Page 32**

A. Answers will vary.

B. 1. When a mother (smokes), she takes a (chance) with her child's (health).

2. Our (social worker) can get (glasses) for people who don't have money.

3. A (nurse) (talks) to (groups) (about) family (health).

4. When I eat well, I feel (fine).

5. I have to quit (smoking), (but) I can't give it up.

C. Discuss your sentence with your instructor.

▶ **Page 33**

B. 1. At a good clinic, all who walk in get help.

2. People hope the doctor can tell them what to do.

3. At the clinic, the doctor helps people get well.

C.

```
            d
            o
c  l  i  n  i  c
            t
      h  o  p  e
            r
```

D. 1. doctor
2. clinic
3. hopes

E. Discuss your sentence with your instructor.

▶ **Page 34**

B. 1. The woman said her hand wasn't mending.

2. What can she do about this problem?

3. The nurse can tell the woman what to do.

4. The nurse can help her work on the problem.

C. said, problem, what

D. 1. problems
2. what
3. said

E. Discuss your sentence with your instructor.

▶ **Page 35**

B. 1. Nan wants to see the doctor about her hip.

2. Standing and sitting makes her hip feel bad.

3. The doctor wants Nan to walk more.

4. He said more walking is good for her hip.

C.

D. 1. hip
2. want
3. more

E. Discuss your sentence with your instructor.

▶ **Page 36**

A. dip, nip, rip, zip

B. 1. The nurse has lots of health (tips).

2. When the child fell down, he cut his (lip).

3. A (sip) of cold water will help.

C. Discuss your sentence with your instructor.

D. 1. X̶ N I P Ȳ̶   nip *or* tip

2. Ɫ̶ C̶ L I P   lip *or* clip

3. T M X̶ I P   tip *or* rip

4. [S] [H] [I] [P] [Z]   hip *or* ship
5. [G] [A] [Z] [I] [P]

►Page 37
A. lope, mope, pope
B. 1. Jan feels that she has no (hope) of getting well.
   2. She sits in bed and (mopes) about her problems.
   3. Jan can't (cope) with bad health.
   4. I (hope) that Jan will get well.
C. Discuss your sentence with your instructor.
D. 1. cope
   2. rope

► Page 38
A. 1. buyer
   2. helper
   3. reader
   4. smoker
   5. talker
   6. player
C. 1. smoker
   2. helper
   3. reader
   4. talker

► Page 41
Think About It
Discuss your answers with your instructor.
1. The doctor treats patients. She works with nurses and social workers, and she keeps a daily log.
2. The doctor uses a daily log as a record of clinic work and daily problems.
3. Answers will vary.
4. Summaries should include the idea that the doctor treats patients for physical

problems, refers some patients to self-help groups or social services, and works with social workers and with patients' families.
Write About It
Discuss your writing with your instructor.

Unit 4

► Page 44
A. Answers will vary.
B. 1. (All) (our) (friends) stop by the (lot) to see the (fun).
   2. (All) (nine) of us (love) to get (out) and (play).
   3. We get (lucky) sometimes and win.
   4. We have (fun) when we (play).
   5. (Our) (boss) (got) the (lot) for the (nine) of us to use.
C. Discuss your sentence with your instructor.

► Page 45
B. 1. Someone said that Jan is good at baseball.
   2. Our team needs nine top players to win.
   3. Has Jan played baseball on a men's team?
   4. The boss said that Jan will need our help.
C. need, team, baseball
D. 1. team
   2. baseball
   3. need
E. Discuss your sentence with your instructor.

► Page 46
B. 1. We're going to the game to see Jan play.
   2. It does look like she will be a good player.
   3. She will get to be tops at this game one day.
   4. The team does need her help.

C.

e	h	p	d	a	y	j
q	w	u	o	z	v	l
p	l	q	e	p	i	d
r	z	d	s	k	b	c
m	g	a	m	e	j	h

D. 1. does

2. game

3. day

E. Discuss your sentence with your instructor.

▶ **Page 47**

B. 1. There was going to be a big <u>game</u> at the lot.

2. Jan had to mend the rips in an old <u>uniform</u>.

3. Jan was feeling fine <u>because</u> she played well.

C.

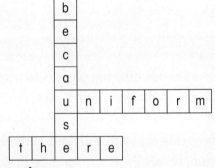

D. 1. there

2. because

3. uniform

E. Discuss your sentence with your instructor.

▶ **Page 48**

A. hay, Jay, lay, ray, say

B. 1. This (may) be our lucky (day).

2. (Lay) down the bat and run, (Ray)!

3. That's the (way) to (play) this game!

C. Discuss your sentence with your instructor.

D. 1. Ⓞ H A Y X E

2. X X P A Y Ⓤ pay *or* Ray

3. X Ⓒ X S A Y

4. J A Y X X Ⓦ

5. X C L A Y X clay *or* lay

▶ **Page 49**

A. reed, seed, weed

B. 1. The players (need) to have some fun.

2. I can (feed) the baseball team at my home.

3. That will be my good (deed) for the team.

C. Discuss your sentence with your instructor.

D. 1. weeds

2. need

3. feed

4. Heed

▶ **Page 50**

A. 1. The Lake City team didn't have a woman player.

2. Did they want Jan?

3. You bet they did!

B. Discuss your sentences with your instructor.

▶ **Page 53**

<u>Think About It</u>

Discuss your answers with your instructor.

1. Three men on the team got sick.

2. The women wanted to play baseball with people who wanted them on the team.

3. They decided the women should be on the team when they saw that the women were good players.

4. Summaries should include the idea that the men at first did not want to let a lot of women onto the team, but, after they saw how good the women were, they changed their minds.

Write About It
Discuss your writing with your instructor.

Unit 5

▶ **Page 56**

A. Answers will vary.

B. I. (My) (dog) wants to (do) well, but
   sometimes he makes (mistakes).

   2. (His) (eyes) shine with pride when he (does)
   well.

   3. Sundown likes to (eat), and he will (be)
   (fed) two times a day.

   4. (Did) Sundown (eat) all (his) food?

   5. I (send) (my) (dog) out to play when (his)
   work ends.

C. Discuss your sentence with your instructor.

▶ **Page 57**

B. I. Not all prisons give people a chance
   like this.

   2. The dogs we teach will help people
   someday.

   3. The dogs learn to work with people who
   need them.

   4. I hope I can use this prison job when
   I get out.

C.

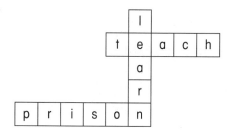

D. I. teach
   2. learning
   3. prison

E. Discuss your sentence with your instructor.

▶ **Page 58**

B. I. We teach our dogs to do different things.

   2. These dogs are helpers for disabled
   people.

   3. People have different needs for our dogs.

   4. Dogs help disabled people to get out.

C. disabled, things, different

D. I. different, things
   2. disabled

E. Discuss your sentence with your instructor.

▶ **Page 59**

B. I. June had to learn to work with her dog.

   2. She learned the right way to tell the dog
   what to do.

   3. The dog comes when June calls it.

   4. June has the right dog for her needs.

C.

s	w	d	a	l	c	n
f	l	p	c	k	o	y
r	i	g	h	t	m	b
a	k	j	u	n	e	x
z	q	b	f	p	d	v

D. I. right
   2. June
   3. come

E. Discuss your sentence with your instructor.

▶ **Page 60**

A. light, might, tight

B. I. Our dogs help people with bad (sight).

   2. They are on the job day and (night).

   3. Disabled people need to find a dog that
   is (right) for them.

C. Discuss your sentence with your instructor.

D. I. 🔲 F I G H T 🔲

   2. 🔲 🔲 M I G H T

3. ⬜L⬜ ⬜I⬜ ⬜G⬜ ⬜H⬜ ⬜T⬜ ⊠ ⊠

4. ⊠ ⬜T⬜ ⬜I⬜ ⬜G⬜ ⬜H⬜ ⬜T⬜ ⊠

5. ⊠ ⊠ ⬜N⬜ ⬜I⬜ ⬜G⬜ ⬜H⬜ ⬜T⬜

▶ Page 61

A. cute, lute, mute

B. 1. Some disabled people can't talk. They are (mute).

2. (June) has trouble getting about in the city because she can't see.

3. Her dog may be (cute), but it isn't a pet.

C. Discuss your sentence with your instructor.

D. 1. tune   2. dunes
   3. mute   4. cute

▶ Page 62

A. came, said, was, were, went, took, gave, fed

C. 1. did, was
   2. were
   3. gave

▶ Page 65

Think About It

Discuss your answers with your instructor.

1. She learned to train dogs to help disabled people.

2. She grows to love them and is sad to see them go.

3. June's life became better when she got Sundown. He helped her become more independent.

4. Summaries should include the idea that Fay put her prison time to good use, and became more hopeful about her future. They may also include the idea that June became more hopeful about her future after she got Sundown.

Write About It

Discuss your writing with your instructor.

Unit 6

▶ Page 68

A. Answers will vary.

B. 1. I (bet) I won't make it home (on) the (holidays).

2. My (son) (will) be (upset) about that.

3. I (bet) a job with a (bigger) store (will) (fit) my needs.

4. I (read) the (ads) , but there are (no) jobs for someone like me.

5. Maybe my friend Bill (will) give me a (hand).

C. Discuss your sentence with your instructor.

▶ Page 69

B. 1. In my job I'm on the road day and night.

2. When I drive my rig, I have my C.B. radio on all the time.

3. I talk to people like me who are on the road.

4. I'm lucky to own the rig I drive.

C. rig, road, drive

D. 1. road
   2. drive
   3. rig

E. Discuss your sentence with your instructor.

▶ Page 70

B. 1. The more I carry, the more money I can make.

2. This time my truck will carry heavy goods.

3. When I carry heavy goods, I need more time to get there.

4. It's a big job to drive a heavy truck.

C.

q	j	t	r	u	c	k
z	g	p	l	i	a	f
v	f	d	y	l	r	m
x	k	q	l	s	r	x
l	h	e	a	v	y	z

D. 1. truck
2. heavy
3. carry

E. Discuss your sentence with your instructor.

▶ **Page 71**

B. 1. On <u>cold</u> days like this, I get <u>lonely</u>.
2. On good days, I don't <u>mind</u> being on the road.
3. It's a <u>lonely</u> job to drive a heavy rig all day.
4. Hope and the children are on my <u>mind</u>.

C.

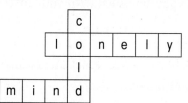

D. 1. mind
2. cold
3. lonely

E. Discuss your sentence with your instructor.

▶ **Page 72**

A. fig, pig, wig

B. 1. Some truckers carry (pigs) in from the country.
2. Can I learn to drive a heavy (rig)?
3. My son wants to drive a truck when he gets (big).

C. Discuss your sentence with your instructor.

D. 1. ☒ R I G ☒
2. ☒ ☒ W I G

3. P I G ☒ ☒
4. ☒ D I G ☒

▶ **Page 73**

A. bold, gold, hold, mold, told

B. 1. It's (cold) and lonely on the road.
2. I'll (hold) on to the job because it pays well.
3. I hope the rig won't be (sold).

C. Discuss your sentence with your instructor.

D. 1. gold
2. cold
3. told
4. sold

▶ **Page 74**

A. 1. faked, faking
2. liked, liking
3. loved, loving
4. timed, timing
5. tuned, tuning
6. used, using

C. 1. loved
2. tuning
3. timing

▶ **Page 77**

Think About It

Discuss your answers with your instructor.

1. He misses them and wants to get news from home.
2. She has to handle the children's illnesses, accidents, and general care.
3. Dell likes making good money, but sometimes feels lonely. His family wishes he worked closer to home.
4. Summaries should include the idea that Dell and Hope dislike being separated so

much, but they both accept Dell's way of making a living.

Write About It

Discuss your writing with your instructor.

Unit 7

▶ **Page 80**

A. Answers will vary.

B. 1. (Parents) are upset (about) the (safety) of the (children) who (play) in this lot.

   2. Can you (see) all the glass and weeds (there)?

   3. It's not (right) to let (children) (play) where they might get (hurt).

   4. I (hope) someone can do something (about) the problem.

   5. I (want) to be the (person) who helps.

C. Discuss your sentence with your instructor.

▶ **Page 81**

B. 1. You need a good <u>camera</u> to take good <u>photos</u>.

   2. I used to take a lot of <u>photos</u> of my children.

   3. Getting children to sit <u>still</u> for a <u>photo</u> is a problem.

   4. My children are older, but I <u>still</u> take a lot of <u>photos</u>.

C.

v	o	t	j	m	i	c	s
b	s	g	x	q	i	l	t
q	c	a	m	e	r	a	i
n	p	h	o	t	o	i	l
p	k	f	d	v	z	a	l

D. 1. camera

   2. photos

   3. still

E. Discuss your sentence with your instructor.

▶ **Page 82**

B. 1. This <u>street</u> sees a lot of <u>action</u>.

   2. The lot at the end of the <u>street</u> is a big problem.

   3. We want <u>action</u>, but the talking <u>drags</u> on and on.

C.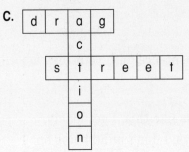

D. 1. street

   2. drag

   3. action

E. Discuss your sentence with your instructor.

▶ **Page 83**

B. 1. <u>Many</u> parents are upset about the safety of the children.

   2. No one can <u>beat</u> a group of parents who are upset.

   3. <u>Together</u> they can make the city do something.

   4. When parents stand <u>together</u>, they can <u>beat</u> a problem.

C. beat, together, many

D. 1. many

   2. together

   3. beat

E. Discuss your sentence with your instructor.

▶ **Page 84**

A. gag, lag, nag, tag, wag

B. 1. Rosa has to carry a heavy camera (bag).

   2. She (drags) it with her all the time.

3. Sometimes Rosa (lags) behind us to take a photo.

4. Don't (nag) Rosa if she takes a lot of photos.

C. Discuss your sentence with your instructor.

D. 1. ~~O~~ T A G ~~K~~
   2. G A G ~~K~~ ~~U~~
   3. ~~O~~ ~~X~~ W A G
   4. ~~L~~ R A G ~~H~~ rag *or* lag

▶ **Page 85**

A. feat, seat, meat, wheat

B. 1. The lot has to be safe and (neat) .
   2. Do you feel the city will (treat) us right?
   3. City Hall can (seat) many people.
   4. Together we make the city feel the (heat) .

C. Discuss your sentence with your instructor.

D. 1. wheat
   2. beats
   3. heat
   4. neat

▶ **Page 86**

B. 1. Will said, "Can I help you carry that heavy camera?"
   2. "It isn't heavy to me," said Rosa.
   3. "Let me use the camera to take a photo," said Will.

▶ **Page 89**

Think About It

Discuss your answers with your instructor.

1. She wanted to show how unsafe the lot was for children.

2. She learned that one person can't do it all and that people have to stand together.

3. Answers will vary.

4. Summaries should include the idea that Rosa took action to get something productive done. She may be headed for a career as a professional photographer.

Write About It

Discuss your writing with your instructor.

Unit 1 Review
▶ **Page 90**

A. 1. sells, records   2. tapes
   3. down   4. value

B. 1. sell *or* sake; sell
   2. well *or* wake; well
   3. tell *or* take; take
   4. make; make

C. 1. sometimes   2. upset
   3. downhill   4. workout
   5. videotapes

Unit 2 Review
▶ **Page 91**

A. 1. parents, give   2. own, life
   3. social worker   4. hug, when

B. 1. hug; hug   2. rug; rug
   3. fine; fine   4. nine; nine

C. 1. woman   2. children
   3. These   4. men

Unit 3 Review
▶ **Page 92**

A. 1. doctor, clinic   2. said, problem
   3. hope, more   4. want, hip

B. 1. hip *or* hope; hip
   2. tip; tip
   3. hope *or* hip; hope
   4. cope; cope

C. 1. helper   2. player

3. worker   4. smoker

5. reader

Unit 4 Review

▶ **Page 93**

A. 1. need; baseball; team

2. game; day

3. does; because

4. There; uniform

B. 1. need; need

2. feed; feed

3. say *or* seed; say

4. may; may

C. 1. Jan ran to the base.

2. Will she make it home?

3. What a hit!

4. Did they win?

5. No way!

6. Can women play baseball as well as men?

Unit 5 Review

▶ **Page 94**

A. 1. prison, learn, teach   2. come, right

3. disabled   4. different

B. 1. might; might   2. sight; sight

3. fight; fight   4. June; June

C. 1. come — did

2. do — were

3. is — went

4. are — came

5. go — gave

6. give — was

Unit 6 Review

▶ **Page 95**

A. 1. drive; rig *or* truck; road

2. truck *or* rig, heavy; carry

3. cold; lonely

4. mind

B. 1. rig; rig

2. big *or* bold; big

3. cold; cold

4. sold; sold

C. 1. liked, liking

2. loved, loving

3. smoked, smoking

4. taped, taping

5. timed, timing

6. used, using

Unit 7 Review

▶ **Page 96**

A. 1. camera

2. Many; action

3. together; street

4. still; photos

B. 1. bag *or* beat; bag

2. tag; tag

3. heat; heat

4. beat *or* bag; beat

C. 1. "I will help you with that heavy bag," said Will.

2. Rosa said, "It's not as heavy as it looks."

3. "I can see you are good at taking photos," said Will.

Word List
● ● ● ● ●

Below is a list of the 195 words that are presented to students in *Book Three* of *Reading for Today*. These words are introduced on sight word, phonics, and language pages. The words will be reviewed in later books. Students should also be familiar with other words based on the phonetically regular spellings of long and short vowel sounds in the consonant-vowel-consonant (CVC) and consonant-vowel-consonant + silent *e* (CVC+ *e*) patterns.

A
action

B
bag
bake
baseball
beat
because
bell
bold
bug
buyer

C
came
camera
carry
child
clay
clinic
clip
cold
come
cope
cute

D
day
deed
Dell
different
dig
dine
dip
disabled
doctor
does
down
downhill
drag
drive
dug
dune

F
fake
faked
faking
feat
feed
fell
fig
fight
fine
fold

G
gag
game
gave
give
gold

H
hay
heat
heavy
heed
helper
hip
hold
hope
hoped
hoping
hug

J
Jay
jug
June

L
lag
lake
lay
learn
leaves
life
liked
liking
line
lip
lives
lonely
lope
loved
loving
lug
lute

M
make
many
may
meat
men
might
mind
mine
mold
mope
more
mug
mute

N
nag
neat
need
Nell
night
nip

O
outlet
own

P

parents
person
photo
pig
pine
player
pope
prison
problem
prune

R

rag
rake
ray
reader
records
reed
rig
right
rip
road
rope
rug

S

sag
said
sake
say
seat

see
seed
sell
shake
shell
shine
ship
shop
sight
sip
smoker
social worker
sold
sometimes
still
street

T

tag
take
talker
tapes
teach
team
tell
there
these
things
tight
time
timed
timing

tip
together
told
took
treat
truck
tug
tune
tuned
tuning

U

uniform
used
using

V

value
video
videotape
vine

W

wag
wake
want
way
weed
were
what
wheat
when

whine
who
wig
wine
women
worker
workout

Z

zip